THE
DEATH PENALTY
OPPOSING VIEWPOINTS

Other Books of Related Interest in the Opposing
Viewpoints Series:

American Values
America's Prisons
Civil Liberties
Crime and Criminals
Criminal Justice
Poverty
Racism in America
Social Justice
Terrorism
Violence in America
War on Drugs

THE DEATH PENALTY
OPPOSING VIEWPOINTS

David L. Bender & Bruno Leone, *Series Editors*

Carol Wekesser, *Book Editor*

OPPOSING VIEWPOINTS SERIES ®

Greenhaven Press, Inc.   PO Box 289009   San Diego, CA 92198-9009

Library of Congress Cataloging-in-Publication Data

The Death penalty : opposing viewpoints / Carol Wekesser, book editor.
   p.   cm. — (Opposing viewpoints series)
  Includes bibliographical references and index.
  Summary: Opposing viewpoints debate death penalty issues. Includes critical thinking activities.
  ISBN 0-89908-180-0 (library binding). — ISBN 0-89908-155-X (pbk.)
  1. Capital punishment. [1. Capital punishment. 2. Critical thinking.] I. Wekesser, Carol, 1963- . II. Series: Opposing viewpoints series (Unnumbered)
HV8694.D385 1991
364.6'6—dc20

                                                            91-9931

"Congress shall make no law . . . abridging the freedom of speech, or of the press."

First Amendment to the U.S. Constitution

The basic foundation of our democracy is the first amendment guarantee of freedom of expression. The Opposing Viewpoints Series is dedicated to the concept of this basic freedom and the idea that it is more important to practice it than to enshrine it.

Contents

Page

Why Consider Opposing Viewpoints?   9

Introduction   12

Chapter 1: Three Centuries of Debate on the Death Penalty

Chapter Preface   16

1. The Death Penalty Will Discourage Crime (1701)   17
   Paper Presented Before the English Parliament

2. The Death Penalty Will Not Discourage Crime (1764)   21
   Cesare Beccaria

3. Society Must Retain the Death Penalty for Murder (1868)   27
   John Stuart Mill

4. The Death Penalty Is State-Sanctioned Murder (1872)   35
   Horace Greeley

5. Capital Punishment Is a Safeguard for Society (1925)   41
   Robert E. Crowe

6. Capital Punishment Will Not Safeguard Society (1928)   47
   Clarence Darrow

A Critical Thinking Activity: 53
   Evaluating Sources of Information

Chapter 2: Is the Death Penalty Just?

Chapter Preface   56

1. The Death Penalty Is Just   57
   Jacob Sullum

2. The Death Penalty Is Unjust   61
   Lloyd Steffen

3. Christians Can Morally Support the Death Penalty   67
   Michael Pakaluk

4. Christians Cannot Morally Support the Death Penalty   74
   John Dear

5. Executing Juvenile Murderers Is Just   82
   Ernest van den Haag

6. Executing Juvenile Murderers Is Unjust   86
   Glenn M. Bieler

A Critical Thinking Activity: 91
  Determining a Punishment for Murder
Periodical Bibliography   94

Chapter 3: Is the Death Penalty an Effective Punishment?

Chapter Preface   96
1. The Death Penalty Is an Effective Punishment   97
  Robert W. Lee
2. The Death Penalty Is Not an Effective Punishment   105
  Matthew L. Stephens
3. The Death Penalty Deters Murder   113
  Steven Goldberg
4. The Death Penalty Does Not Deter Murder   119
  Stephen Nathanson
5. Limitless Appeals Make the Death Penalty Ineffective   127
  William H. Rehnquist
6. Limiting Death Sentence Appeals Would Harm Civil Rights   133
  Stephen Reinhardt
A Critical Thinking Activity: 137
  Distinguishing Between Fact and Opinion
Periodical Bibliography   139

Chapter 4: Does the Death Penalty Discriminate?

Chapter Preface   141
1. The Death Penalty Discriminates Against Blacks   142
  Anthony G. Amsterdam
2. The Death Penalty Does Not Discriminate Against Blacks   148
  Laurence W. Johnson
3. The Death Penalty Discriminates Against the Poor   152
  Michael E. Endres
4. Guilt Overrides the Importance of Death Penalty Discrimination   156
  Ernest van den Haag
A Critical Thinking Activity: 160
  Understanding Words in Context
Periodical Bibliography   162

Chapter 5: Do Certain Crimes Deserve the Death Penalty?

Chapter Preface   164
1. Drug Dealers Should Be Executed   165
  Alfonse D'Amato & William F. Buckley Jr.

2. Drug Dealers Should Not Be Executed   169
   Sandra R. Acosta
3. Terrorists Should Be Executed   174
   Robert A. Friedlander
4. Terrorists Should Not Be Executed   178
   Amnesty International

A Critical Thinking Activity: 182
   Distinguishing Bias from Reason

Organizations to Contact   184
Bibliography of Books   187
Index   188

Why Consider Opposing Viewpoints?

"It is better to debate a question without settling it than to settle a question without debating it."

Joseph Joubert (1754-1824)

The Importance of Examining Opposing Viewpoints

The purpose of the Opposing Viewpoints Series, and this book in particular, is to present balanced, and often difficult to find, opposing points of view on complex and sensitive issues.

Probably the best way to become informed is to analyze the positions of those who are regarded as experts and well studied on issues. It is important to consider every variety of opinion in an attempt to determine the truth. Opinions from the mainstream of society should be examined. But also important are opinions that are considered radical, reactionary, or minority as well as those stigmatized by some other uncomplimentary label. An important lesson of history is the eventual acceptance of many unpopular and even despised opinions. The ideas of Socrates, Jesus, and Galileo are good examples of this.

Readers will approach this book with their own opinions on the issues debated within it. However, to have a good grasp of one's own viewpoint, it is necessary to understand the arguments of those with whom one disagrees. It can be said that those who do not completely understand their adversary's point of view do not fully understand their own.

A persuasive case for considering opposing viewpoints has been presented by John Stuart Mill in his work *On Liberty*. When examining controversial issues it may be helpful to reflect on this suggestion:

The only way in which a human being can make some approach to knowing the whole of a subject, is by hearing what
can be said about it by persons of every variety of opinion,
and studying all modes in which it can be looked at by every
character of mind. No wise man ever acquired his wisdom in
any mode but this.

Analyzing Sources of Information

The Opposing Viewpoints Series includes diverse materials
taken from magazines, journals, books, and newspapers, as well
as statements and position papers from a wide range of individuals, organizations, and governments. This broad spectrum of
sources helps to develop patterns of thinking which are open to
the consideration of a variety of opinions.

Pitfalls to Avoid

A pitfall to avoid in considering opposing points of view is that
of regarding one's own opinion as being common sense and the
most rational stance, and the point of view of others as being
only opinion and naturally wrong. It may be that another's
opinion is correct and one's own is in error.

Another pitfall to avoid is that of closing one's mind to the
opinions of those with whom one disagrees. The best way to approach a dialogue is to make one's primary purpose that of understanding the mind and arguments of the other person and
not that of enlightening him or her with one's own solutions.
More can be learned by listening than speaking.

It is my hope that after reading this book the reader will have
a deeper understanding of the issues debated and will appreciate the complexity of even seemingly simple issues on which
good and honest people disagree. This awareness is particularly
important in a democratic society such as ours where people enter into public debate to determine the common good. Those
with whom one disagrees should not necessarily be regarded as
enemies, but perhaps simply as people who suggest different
paths to a common goal.

Developing Basic Reading and Thinking Skills

In this book, carefully edited opposing viewpoints are purposely placed back to back to create a running debate; each
viewpoint is preceded by a short quotation that best expresses
the author's main argument. This format instantly plunges the
reader into the midst of a controversial issue and greatly aids
that reader in mastering the basic skill of recognizing an author's point of view.

A number of basic skills for critical thinking are practiced in
the activities that appear throughout the books in the series.
Some of the skills are:

Evaluating Sources of Information. The ability to choose from among alternative sources the most reliable and accurate source in relation to a given subject.

Separating Fact from Opinion. The ability to make the basic distinction between factual statements (those that can be demonstrated or verified empirically) and statements of opinion (those that are beliefs or attitudes that cannot be proved).

Identifying Stereotypes. The ability to identify oversimplified, exaggerated descriptions (favorable or unfavorable) about people and insulting statements about racial, religious, or national groups, based upon misinformation or lack of information.

Recognizing Ethnocentrism. The ability to recognize attitudes or opinions that express the view that one's own race, culture, or group is inherently superior, or those attitudes that judge another culture or group in terms of one's own.

It is important to consider opposing viewpoints and equally important to be able to critically analyze those viewpoints. The activities in this book are designed to help the reader master these thinking skills. Statements are taken from the book's viewpoints and the reader is asked to analyze them. This technique aids the reader in developing skills that not only can be applied to the viewpoints in this book, but also to situations where opinionated spokespersons comment on controversial issues. Although the activities are helpful to the solitary reader, they are most useful when the reader can benefit from the interaction of group discussion.

Using this book and others in the series should help readers develop basic reading and thinking skills. These skills should improve the reader's ability to understand what is read. Readers should be better able to separate fact from opinion, substance from rhetoric, and become better consumers of information in our media-centered culture.

This volume of the Opposing Viewpoints Series does not advocate a particular point of view. Quite the contrary! The very nature of the book leaves it to the reader to formulate the opinions he or she finds most suitable. My purpose as publisher is to see that this is made possible by offering a wide range of viewpoints that are fairly presented.

David L. Bender
Publisher

Introduction

"It is but law that when the red drops have been spilled upon the ground they cry aloud for fresh blood."

Aeschylus, *Libation Bearers* (458 BC)

"Our ancestors . . . purged their guilt by banishment, not death. And by so doing, they stopped that endless vicious cycle of murder and revenge."

Euripides, *Orestes* (408 BC)

Legal execution—society's ultimate sanction—has existed as long as has human culture. One of the first written codes of law, composed by Hammurabi of Babylonia and carved on a stone column nearly four thousand years ago, includes death as an appropriate punishment. In most cultures, this sentence is reserved for the most severe crimes—murder, violent sexual assault, and treason. But in some times and places, in both simple and sophisticated societies, punishments for many crimes have been startlingly severe, even including death for stealing a loaf of bread or writing derogatory songs about notables.

Today more than one-half of the world's nations use capital punishment—some commonly, some infrequently. Iran, for example, was the site of more than 740 legal executions between 1985 and 1988. In Ireland capital punishment is legal, but the last state-sanctioned execution was in 1954. In the United States capital punishment is legal in about two-thirds of the states, but its actual imposition occurs only rarely and only after lengthy, automatic processes of legal appeals.

Even in some countries that have abolished the death penalty for most offenses, there are crimes for which they continue to use this ultimate punishment. In Morocco, attempted assassination of the king, murder, and arson are capital crimes. Israel has retained it for treason, war crimes, and acts of terrorism. The legislative bodies of these countries believe that some crimes call for death as just punishment or retribution for the crime committed or as a deterrent to future crimes of a similar nature.

A few countries, notably Sweden, Denmark, Finland, and

Portugal, have not allowed capital punishment for decades. The United Nations urges the worldwide abolition of capital punishment on the grounds that "every human has an inherent right to life." Numerous individual countries have also been moving in this direction. Canada abolished the death penalty in 1976. Since 1981, it is no longer possible in France for criminals to be executed, a fact deplored by many of those who believe that death is a just and effective punishment but applauded by those who regard such executions as barbaric and immoral. Despite a dramatic rise in terrorism and violent crime, Britain's parliament has voted several times not to reinstate the death penalty, abolished in 1965.

U.S. States That Have Abolished the Death Penalty

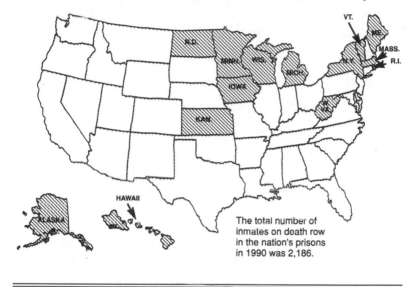

The total number of inmates on death row in the nation's prisons in 1990 was 2,186.

While some cheer the move to abolish capital punishment, others are convinced that it is a necessary weapon for society to defend itself. The relatively recent phenomenon of vicious serial murders and the alarming increase in world terrorism are two of the extreme trends to which supporters of the death penalty point. These crimes seem to many to require the certainty of the most severe form of retaliation in order to increase the risk for the murderers and possibly reduce it for the rest of society.

The Death Penalty: Opposing Viewpoints replaces Greenhaven Press's 1986 volume of the same title. It includes ideas drawn from the works of philosophers, judges, criminologists, attorneys, religious leaders, government officials, journalists, and human rights organizations. The viewpoints in this book focus on several of the most discussed issues in the capital punishment debate. Chapter titles include: Three Centuries of Debate on the Death Penalty, Is the Death Penalty Just? Is the Death Penalty an Effective Punishment? Does the Death Penalty Discriminate? Do Certain Crimes Deserve the Death Penalty? As with all volumes in the Opposing Viewpoints series, the opinions of these authors are presented without editorial comment or interference. Readers, therefore, are left to analyze and evaluate the arguments about this controversial issue and to draw their own conclusions.

Three Centuries of Debate
on the Death Penalty

Chapter Preface

Controversy over the death penalty is recent in the history of humankind. Most ancient societies accepted the idea that certain crimes deserved capital punishment. Ancient Roman and Mosaic law endorsed the notion of retaliation; they believed in the rule of "an eye for an eye." Similarly, the ancient Egyptians, Assyrians, and Greeks all executed citizens for a variety of offenses, ranging from perjury to murder.

Adherence to the death penalty continued into the Middle Ages, during which religious crimes such as sacrilege, heresy, and atheism were punishable by death. European settlers brought the death penalty to the American colonies, where idolatry, witchcraft, blasphemy, murder, sodomy, adultery, rape, perjury, and rebellion were all capital crimes in 1636. This continuing use of the death penalty reflected society's belief that severe crimes warranted severe punishments and that such punishments would deter others from committing such crimes.

This view was challenged during the Enlightenment of the eighteenth century, which dramatically altered European and American perceptions about political and social issues such as capital punishment. A movement to abolish or at least restrict the death penalty began to take shape in the writings of Cesare Beccaria, Montesquieu, Voltaire, and others. Their views were reflected in the words of American revolutionary Benjamin Rush in 1792: "The punishment of murder by death is contrary to reason, and to the order and happiness of society." Some European leaders banned the death penalty. One such leader, Catherine the Great of Russia, stated, "There can be no necessity for taking away the life of a citizen."

Other philosophers of this period, however, defended the death penalty. German philosopher Immanuel Kant asserted that the death penalty was the most equitable punishment for murder. Unremorseful murderers deserve to die, he believed, while remorseful, guilt-ridden murderers would welcome death as a relief from their emotional pain. The United States and most European nations continued to execute criminals, believing in its justness and in its deterrent effect.

Eighteenth-century philosophers such as Kant and Beccaria sparked a controversy that continued into the nineteenth and twentieth centuries. The following chapter presents a variety of historical arguments supporting and opposing the death penalty.

"Those who shew no mercy should find none; and if Hanging will not restrain them, Hanging them in Chains, and Starving them, or . . . breaking them on the Wheel . . . should."

The Death Penalty Will Discourage Crime (1701)

Paper Presented Before the English Parliament

In eighteenth-century England, some two hundred crimes were punishable by death, including pickpocketing and petty theft. Many people were attempting to reform this excess of executions by reducing the sentences for many offenses. Others believed, however, that the death penalty should continue to be rigorously applied for heinous crimes. In the following viewpoint, the author states that punishments should remain severe and perhaps be even more so. He argues that keeping the death penalty a very real threat is the only way to stop people from committing violent and offensive crimes.

As you read, consider the following questions:

1. Why does the author believe the death penalty must be used "steadily and impartially"?
2. On what does the author base his argument that there should be differences in the degrees of punishments?
3. What does the author say society should be careful of when applying the death penalty?

Hanging Not Punishment Enough for Murtherers, Highway Men, and House-Breakers. London: A. Balwin, 1701.

I am sensible, That the *English* Clemency and Mildness appear eminently in our Laws and Constitutions; but since it is found that *Ill* Men are grown so much more incorrigible, than in our fore-fathers Days, is it not fit that *Good* Men should grow less merciful to them, since gentler Methods are ineffectual?

I acknowledge also, That the Spirit of Christianity disposes us to Patience and Forbearance, insomuch that when the *Roman* Emperors began to grow Christian, we are informed, That most Capital Punishments were taken away, and turned into others less Sanguinary; either that they might have longer time for Repentance, (an Indulgence agreeable to the Zeal and Piety of those Good Ages) or that the length and continuance of their Punishment might be more Exemplary. And I acknowledge with the Wise *Quintilian, That if Ill men could be made Good, as, it must be granted, they sometimes may, it is for the Interest of the Commonwealth, that they should rather be spared than punished.* And I know, that 'tis frequently alledg'd, That you take away a Better thing, and that is a Man's Life, for that which is worse, and that is, your Money and Goods; but tho' this be speciously enough urged, yet I doubt not, but the Publick Safety and Happiness may lawfully and reasonably be secured by this way, if it can by no other. . . .

Show No Mercy to the Merciless

I must beg leave to say, that those who shew no mercy should find none; and if Hanging will not restrain them, Hanging them in Chains, and Starving them, or (if Murtherers and Robbers at the same time, or Night incendiaries) breaking them on the Wheel, or Whipping them to Death, a *Roman* Punishment should.

I know that Torments so unusual and unknown to us may at first surprize us, and appear unreasonable; but I hope easily to get over that difficulty, and make it appear upon Examination, that *that* will be the more probable way to secure us from our fears of them, and the means of preserving great numbers of them, who now yearly by an easie Death are taken off at the Gallows. For to Men so far corrupted in their Principles and Practices, and that have no expectations beyond the Grave (for such, I fear, is the case of most of them) no Argument will be so cogent, as Pain in an intense degree; and a few such Examples made, will be so terrifying, that I persuade myself it would be a Law but seldom put in Execution.

The Death Penalty Must Be Used

But then I must add, that I fear it will not have its due effects, if it be too often dispens'd with; since *that* will be apt to give ground to every Offender, to hope he may be of the number of *those*, who shall escape, and so the good end of the Law will be defeated. For if Favour or Affection, or a Man's being of a good

18

Family, or Money can prevail, and take off the Penalty of the Statute; if it be not executed steadily and impartially, with an exact hand (still giving allowance for extraordinary Cases) it will serve to little purpose, since many will be found (as ill men easily flatter themselves) who will not fear a Law, that has sharp Teeth indeed, but does but sometimes bite. And this, I believe, must be allowed to be the only way to root out our Native Enemies, as they truly are; as might lately have been seen in a Neighbouring Kingdom, where severity, without the least mixture of mercy, did so sweep High-way Men out of the Nation, that it has been confidently said, that a Man might some time since have *openly* carried his Money without fear of losing it. That he cannot *now*, is to be charged upon their great numbers of Soldiers, without Employment and Plunder, and in poor pitiful Pay; and, it may be, on the very great necessities of the People, and make 'em desperate and careless of their Lives.

Severe Penalties Prevent Crime

In England, Germany, and France, a man knows, that if he commit murder, every person around him will, from that instant, become his enemy, and use every means to seize him and bring him to justice. He knows that he will be immediately carried to prison, and put to an ignominious death, amidst the execrations of his countrymen. Impressed with these sentiments, and with the natural horror for murder which such sentiments augment, the populace of those countries hardly ever have recourse to stabbing in their accidental quarrels, however they may be inflamed with anger and rage. The lowest black-guard in the streets of London will not draw a knife against an antagonist far superior to himself in strength. He will fight him fairly with his fists as long as he can, and bear the severest drubbing, rather than use a means of defence which is held in detestation by his countrymen, and which would bring him to the gallows.

John Moore, *The Opinions of Different Authors upon the Punishment of Death*, 1812.

'Tis a Rule in Civil Law, and Reason, *That the Punishment should not exceed the fault*. If Death then be due to a Man, who surreptitiously steals the Value of Five Shillings (as it is made by a late Statute) surely *He* who puts me in fear of my Life, and breaks the King's Peace, and it may be, murthers me at last, and burns my House, deserves another sort of Censure; and if the one must die, the other should be made to *feel himself die*. . . .

The frequent Repetitions of the same Crimes, even in defiance of the present Laws in being, is a just ground of enacting somewhat more terrible; and indeed seems to challenge and require it.

Farther still; at the *last great day* doubtless there will be degrees of Torment, proportionable to Mens guilt and sin here; and I can see no reason why we may not imitate the Divine justice, and inflict an Animadversion suitable to such enormous Offenders.

And this, I am persuaded, will best answer the End of Sanguinary Laws, which are not *chiefly* intended to punish the present Criminal, but to hinder others from being so; and on that account Punishments in the Learned Languages are called *Examples*, as being design'd to be such to all mankind. . . .

Careful of Shedding Human Blood

Still I am sensible, that tho' I argue for severity, in general ought to be tender of shedding human blood; For *there is such a Consanguinity and Relation between all mankind that no one ought to hurt another, unless for some good end to be obtain'd.* And *Bodily Punishment*, as the Civilian well observes, *is greater than any Pecuniary mulcts*; and every Man knows that he who loses his Life, is a much greater sufferer than he whose Goods are confiscated, or is Fined in the most unreasonable manner in the World.

But my design is not, that Man's blood *should* be shed, but that it should *not*; and I verily believe, that for *Five* Men Condemned and Executed *now*, you would hardly have *one then*. For those Men out of Terror of such a Law, would ('tis to be hoped) either apply themselves to honest Labour and Industry; or else would remove to our *Plantations*, where they are wanted, and so many useful Hands would not be yearly lost.

But I must add, That *it is not fit, that men in Criminal Causes*, as the Civil Law well directs, *should be condemned, unless the Evidence be clearer than the mid-day Sun*; and no Man should expire in such horrid Agonies, for whose Innocence there is the least pretense.

"The punishment of death has never prevented determined men from injuring society."

The Death Penalty Will Not Discourage Crime (1764)

Cesare Beccaria

An Italian criminologist, Cesare Beccaria lived and died in the 1700s. He influenced local economic reforms and stimulated penal reform throughout Europe. In 1764 he published *An Essay on Crimes and Punishments*, one of the first arguments against capital punishment and inhumane treatment of criminals. In the following viewpoint, Beccaria condemns capital punishment on several grounds, including that it is not a deterrent to crime and is irrevocable.

As you read, consider the following questions:

1. Why does Beccaria believe that the death penalty may be justified if a man is a threat to government?
2. What does an execution inspire in others, according to the author? What does he say about this reaction?
3. What does Beccaria say about life imprisonment?

Cesare Beccaria, *An Essay on Crimes and Punishments*, originally published in London by F. Newberry, 1775.

The useless profusion of punishments, which has never made men better, induces me to enquire, whether the punishment of *death* be really just or useful in a well governed state? What *right*, I ask, have men to cut the throats of their fellow-creatures? Certainly not that on which the sovereignty and laws are founded. The laws, as I have said before, are only the sum of the smallest portions of the private liberty of each individual, and represent the general will, which is the aggregate of that of each individual. Did any one ever give to others the right of taking away his life? Is it possible, that in the smallest portions of the liberty of each, sacrificed to the good of the public, can be contained the greatest of all good, life? If it were so, how shall it be reconciled to the maxim which tells us, that a man has no right to kill himself? Which he certainly must have, if he could give it away to another.

But the punishment of death is not authorized by any right; for I have demonstrated that no such right exists. It is therefore a war of a whole nation against a citizen, whose destruction they consider as necessary, or useful to the general good. But if I can further demonstrate, that it is neither necessary nor useful, I shall have gained the cause of humanity.

Only One Reason for the Death Penalty

The death of a citizen cannot be necessary, but in one case. When, though deprived of his liberty, he has such power and connections as may endanger the security of the nation; when his existence may produce a dangerous revolution in the established form of government. But even in this case, it can only be necessary when a nation is on the verge of recovering or losing its liberty; or in times of absolute anarchy, when the disorders themselves hold the place of laws. But in a reign of tranquillity; in a form of government approved by the united wishes of the nation; in a state well fortified from enemies without, and supported by strength within, and opinion, perhaps more efficacious; where all power is lodged in the hands of a true sovereign; where riches can purchase pleasures and not authority, there can be no necessity for taking away the life of a subject.

If the experience of all ages be not sufficient to prove, that the punishment of death has never prevented determined men from injuring society; if the example of the Romans; if twenty years reign of Elizabeth, empress of Russia, in which she gave the fathers of their country an example more illustrious than many conquests bought with blood; if, I say, all this be not sufficient to persuade mankind, who always suspect the voice of reason, and who choose rather to be led by authority, let us consult human nature in proof of my assertion.

It is not the intenseness of the pain that has the greatest effect

22

on the mind, but its continuance; for our sensibility is more easily and more powerfully affected by weak but repeated impressions, than by a violent, but momentary, impulse. The power of habits is universal over every sensible being. As it is by that we learn to speak, to walk, and to satisfy our necessities, so the ideas of morality are stamped on our minds by repeated impressions. The death of a criminal is a terrible but momentary spectacle, and therefore a less efficacious method of deterring others, than the continued example of a man deprived of his liberty, condemned, as a beast of burthen, to repair, by his labour, the injury he has done to society. *If I commit such a crime*, says the spectator to himself, *I shall be reduced to that miserable condition for the rest of my life.* A much more powerful preventive than the fear of death, which men always behold in distant obscurity.

A Dead Man Is Good for Nothing

It hath long since been observed, that a man after he is hanged is good for nothing, and that punishment invented for the good of society, ought to be useful to society. It is evident, that a score of stout robbers, condemned for life to some public work, would serve the state in their punishment, and that hanging them is a benefit to nobody but the executioner.

Commentary on Cesare Beccaria, attributed to Voltaire, c. 1770.

The terrors of death make so slight an impression, that it has not force enough to withstand the forgetfulness natural to mankind, even in the most essential things; especially when assisted by the passions. Violent impressions surprise us, but their effect is momentary; they are fit to produce those revolutions which instantly transform a common man into a Lacedaemonian or a Persian; but in a free and quiet government they ought to be rather frequent than strong.

The execution of a criminal is, to the multitude, a spectacle, which in some excites compassion mixed with indignation. These sentiments occupy the mind much more than that salutary terror which the laws endeavour to inspire; but in the contemplation of continued suffering, terror is the only, or a least predominant sensation. The severity of a punishment should be just sufficient to excite compassion in the spectators, as it is intended more for them than for the criminal.

A punishment, to be just, should have only that degree of severity which is sufficient to deter others. Now there is no man, who upon the least reflection, would put in competition total and perpetual loss of his liberty, with the greatest advan-

23

tages he could possibly obtain in consequence of a crime. Perpetual slavery, then, has in it all that is necessary to deter the most hardened and determined, as much as the punishment of death. I say it has more. There are many who can look upon death with intrepidity and firmness; some through fanaticism, and others through vanity, which attends us even to the grave; others from a desperate resolution, either to get rid of their misery, or cease to live: but fanaticism and vanity forsake the criminal in slavery, in chains and fetters, in an iron cage; and despair seems rather the beginning than the end of their misery. The mind, by collecting itself and uniting all its force, can, for a moment, repel assailing grief; but its most vigorous efforts are insufficient to resist perpetual wretchedness.

In all nations, where death is used as a punishment, every example supposes a new crime committed. Whereas in perpetual slavery, every criminal affords a frequent and lasting example; and if it be necessary that men should often be witnesses of the power of the laws, criminals should often be put to death; but this supposes a frequency of crimes; and from hence this punishment will cease to have its effect, so that it must be useful and useless at the same time.

Slavery and the Death Penalty

I shall be told, that perpetual slavery is as painful a punishment as death, and therefore as cruel. I answer, that if all the miserable moments in the life of a slave were collected into one point, it would be a more cruel punishment than any other; but these are scattered through his whole life, whilst the pain of death exerts all its force in a moment. There is also another advantage in the punishment of slavery, which is, that it is more terrible to the spectator than to the sufferer himself; for the spectator considers the sum of all his wretched moments, whilst the sufferer, by the misery of the present, is prevented from thinking of the future. All evils are increased by the imagination, and the sufferer finds resources and consolations, of which the spectators are ignorant; who judge by their own sensibility of what passes in a mind, by habit grown callous to misfortune.

Let us, for a moment, attend to the reasoning of a robber or assassin, who is deterred from violating the laws by the gibbet or the wheel. I am sensible, that to develop the sentiments of one's own heart, is an art which education only can teach: but although a villain may not be able to give a clear account of his principles, they nevertheless influence his conduct. He reasons thus:

> What are these laws, that I am bound to respect, which make so great a difference between me and the rich man? He refuses me the farthing I ask of him, and excuses himself, by

bidding me have recourse to labour with which he is unacquainted. Who made these laws? The rich and the great, who never deigned to visit the miserable hut of the poor; who have never seen him dividing a piece of mouldly bread, amidst the cries of his famished children and the tears of his wife. Let us break those ties, fatal to the greatest part of mankind, and only useful to a few indolent tyrants. Let us attack injustice at its source. I will return to my natural state of independence. I shall live free and happy on the fruits of my courage and industry. A day of pain and repentance may come, but it will be short; and for an hour of grief I shall enjoy years of pleasure and liberty. King of a small number, as determined as myself, I will correct the mistakes of fortune; and I shall see those tyrants grow pale and tremble at the sight of him, whom, with insulting pride, they would not suffer to rank with their dogs and horses.

Religion then presents itself to the mind of this lawless villain, and promising him almost a certainty of eternal happiness upon the easy terms of repentance, contributes much to lessen the horror of the last scene of the tragedy.

Horrible Punishments Serve No Purpose

A government that persists in retaining these horrible punishments can only assign one reason in justification of their conduct: that they have already so degraded and brutalized the habits of the people, that they cannot be restrained by any moderate punishments.

Are more atrocities committed in those countries where such punishments are unknown? Certainly not: the most savage banditti are always to be found under laws the most severe, and it is no more than what might be expected. The fate with which they are threatened hardens them to the sufferings of others as well as to their own. They know that they can expect no lenity, and they consider their acts of cruelty as retaliations.

Jeremy Bentham, *The Opinions of Different Authors on the Punishment of Death*, 1809.

But he who foresees, that he must pass a great number of years, even his whole life, in pain and slavery; a slave to those laws by which he was protected; in sight of his fellow citizens, with whom he lives in freedom and society; makes an useful comparison between those evils, the uncertainty of his success, and the shortness of the time in which he shall enjoy the fruits of his transgression. The example of those wretches continually before his eyes, make a much greater impression on him than a punishment, which, instead of correcting, makes him more obdurate.

The punishment of death is pernicious to society, from the example of barbarity it affords. If the passions, or the necessity of

25

war, have taught men to shed the blood of their fellow creatures, the laws, which are intended to moderate the ferocity of mankind, should not increase it by examples of barbarity, the more horrible, as this punishment is usually attended with formal pageantry. Is it not absurd, that the laws, which detest and punish homicide, should, in order to prevent murder, publicly commit murder themselves? . . .

Seeking Truth

If it be objected, that almost all the nations in all ages have punished certain crimes with death, I answer, that the force of these examples vanishes, when opposed to truth, against which prescription is urged in vain. The history of mankind is an immense sea of errors, in which a few obscure truths may here and there be found.

But human sacrifices have also been common in almost all nations. That some societies only, either few in number, or for a very short time, abstained from the punishment of death, is rather favourable to my argument, for such is the fate of great truths, that their duration is only as a flash of lightning in the long and dark night of error. The happy time is not yet arrived, when truth, as falsehood has been hitherto, shall be the portion of the greatest number.

> *"We show . . . our regard for [human life] by the adoption of a rule that he who violates that right in another forfeits it for himself."*

Society Must Retain the Death Penalty for Murder (1868)

John Stuart Mill

John Stuart Mill, prominent philosopher and economist, is probably best known as the author of the famous essay *On Liberty*. From 1865 to 1868 he served as a member of the British Parliament and constantly advocated political and social reforms such as emancipation for women, and the development of labor organizations and farm cooperatives. In the following viewpoint, taken from a Parliamentary Debate on April 21, 1868, Mill argues that while he is an advocate for lesser penalties for crimes such as theft, society must retain the death penalty for crimes of murder.

As you read, consider the following questions:

1. Why does the author argue that the death penalty is the most humane alternative for the criminal?
2. Does the death penalty deter crime, according to Mill?
3. Why does the author say he disagrees with the philanthropists on the issue of the death penalty?

John Stuart Mill, *Hansard's Parliamentary Debate*, 3rd Series, London: April 21, 1868.

It is always a matter of regret to me to find myself, on a public question, opposed to those who are called—sometimes in the way of honour, and sometimes in what is intended for ridicule—the philanthropists. Of all persons who take part in public affairs, they are those for whom, on the whole, I feel the greatest amount of respect; for their characteristic is, that they devote their time, their labour, and much of their money to objects purely public, with a less admixture of either personal or class selfishness, than any other class of politicians whatever. On almost all the great questions, scarcely any politicians are so steadily and almost uniformly to be found on the side of right; and they seldom err, but by an exaggerated application of some just and highly important principle. On the very subject that is now occupying us we all know what signal service they have rendered. It is through their efforts that our criminal laws . . . have so greatly relaxed their most revolting and most impolitic ferocity, that aggravated murder is now practically the only crime which is punished with death by any of our lawful tribunals; and we are even now deliberating whether the extreme penalty should be retained in that solitary case. This vast gain, not only to humanity, but to the ends of penal justice, we owe to the philanthropists; and if they are mistaken, as I cannot but think they are, in the present instance, it is only in not perceiving the right time and place for stopping in a career hitherto so eminently beneficial. Sir, there is a point at which, I conceive, that career ought to stop.

Just Penalty for Some Circumstances

When there has been brought home to any one, by conclusive evidence, the greatest crime known to the law; and when the attendant circumstances suggest no palliation of the guilt, no hope that the culprit may even yet not be unworthy to live among mankind, nothing to make it probable that the crime was an exception to his general character rather than a consequence of it, then I confess it appears to me that to deprive the criminal of the life of which he has proved himself to be unworthy— solemnly to blot him out from the fellowship of mankind and from the catalogue of the living—is the most appropriate, as it is certainly the most impressive, mode in which society can attach to so great a crime the penal consequences which for the security of life it is indispensable to annex to it. I defend this penalty, when confined to atrocious cases, on the very ground on which it is commonly attacked—on that of humanity to the criminal; as beyond comparison the least cruel mode in which it is possible adequately to deter from the crime. If, in our horror of inflicting death, we endeavour to devise some punishment for the living criminal which shall act on the human mind with a deterrent force at all comparable to that of death, we are driven to inflictions less severe indeed in appearance, and therefore less efficacious, but far more cruel in reality.

The Most Powerful Deterrent

The punishment of death is unquestionably the most powerful deterrent, the most effective preventive, that can be applied. Human nature teaches this fact. An instinct that outruns all reasoning, a dreadful horror that overcomes all other sentiments, works in us all when we contemplate it.

Samuel Hand, *The North American Review*, December 1881.

Few, I think, would venture to propose, as a punishment for aggravated murder, less than imprisonment with hard labour for life; that is the fate to which a murderer would be consigned by the mercy which shrinks from putting him to death. But has it been sufficiently considered what sort of a mercy this is, and what kind of life it leaves to him? If, indeed, the punishment is not really inflicted—if it becomes the sham which a few years ago such punishments were rapidly becoming—then, indeed, its adoption would be almost tantamount to giving up the attempt to repress murder altogether. But if it really is what it professes to be, and if it is realized in all its rigour by the popular imagination, as it very probably would not be, but as it must be if it is to be efficacious, it will be so shocking that when the memory of the crime is no longer fresh, there will be almost insuperable difficulty in executing it. What comparison can there really be, in point of severity, between consigning a man to the short pang of a rapid death, and immuring him in a living tomb, there to linger out what may be a long life in the hardest and most monotonous toil, without any of its alleviations or rewards—debarred from all pleasant sights and sounds, and cut off from all earthly hope, except a slight mitigation of bodily restraint, or a small improvement of diet? Yet even such a lot as this, because there is no one moment at which the suffering is of terrifying intensity, and, above all, because it does not contain the element, so imposing to the imagination, of the unknown, is universally reputed a milder punishment than death—stands in all codes as a mitigation of the capital penalty, and is thankfully accepted as such. For it is characteristic of all punishments which depend on duration for their efficacy—all, therefore, which are not corporal or pecuniary—that they are more rigorous than they seem; while it is, on the contrary, one of the strongest recommendations a punishment can have, that it should seem more rigorous than it is; for its practical power depends far less on what it is than on what it seems.

There is not, I should think, any human infliction which makes an impression on the imagination so entirely out of proportion to its real severity as the punishment of death. The punishment must be mild indeed which does not add more to the sum of human misery than is necessarily or directly added by the execution of a criminal. . . . The most that human laws can do to anyone in the matter of death is to hasten it; the man would have died at any rate; not so very much later, and on the average, I fear, with a considerably greater amount of bodily suffering. Society is asked, then, to denude itself of an instrument of punishment which, in the grave cases to which alone it is suitable, effects its purpose at a less cost of human suffering than any other; which, while it inspires more terror, is less cruel in actual fact than any punishment that we should think of substituting for it. My hon. Friend [Mr. Gilpin] says that it does not inspire terror, and that experience proves it to be a failure. But the influence of a punishment is not to be estimated by its effect on hardened criminals. Those whose habitual way of life keeps them, so to speak, at all times within sight of the gallows, do grow to care less about it; as, to compare good things with bad, an old soldier is not much affected by the chance of dying in battle. I can afford to admit all that is often said about the indifference of professional criminals to the gallows. Though of that indifference one-third is probably bravado and another third confidence that they shall have the luck to escape, it is quite probable that the remaining third is real. But the efficacy of a punishment which acts principally through the imagination, is chiefly to be measured by the impression it makes on those who are still innocent: by the horror with which it surrounds the first promptings of guilt; the restraining influence it exercises over the beginning of the thought which, if indulged, would become a temptation; the check which it exerts over the gradual declension towards the state—never suddenly attained—in which crime no longer revolts, and punishment no longer terrifies.

Unknown Number of Lives Saved

As for what is called the failure of death punishment, who is able to judge of that? We partly know who those are whom it has not deterred; but who is there who knows whom it has deterred, or how many human beings it has saved who would have lived to be murderers if that awful association had not been thrown round the idea of murder from their earliest infancy? Let us not forget that the most imposing fact loses its power over the imagination if it is made too cheap. When a punishment fit only for the most atrocious crimes is lavished on small offences until human feeling recoils from it, then, indeed, it ceases to intimidate, because it ceases to be believed in.

The failure of capital punishment in cases of theft is easily accounted for: the thief did not believe that it would be inflicted. He had learnt by experience that jurors would perjure themselves rather than find him guilty; that Judges would seize any excuse for not sentencing him to death, or for recommending him to mercy; and that if neither jurors nor Judges were merciful, there were still hopes from an authority above both. When things had come to this pass it was high time to give up the vain attempt. When it is impossible to inflict a punishment, or when its infliction becomes a public scandal, the idle threat cannot too soon disappear from the statute book. And in the case of the host of offences which were formerly capital, I heartily rejoice that it did become impracticable to execute the law.

Deserved Retribution

Capital execution upon the deadly poisoner and the midnight assassin is not only necessary for the safety of society, it is the fit and deserved retribution of their crimes. By it alone is divine and human justice fulfilled.

Samuel Hand, *The North American Review*, December 1881.

If the same state of public feeling comes to exist in the case of murder; if the time comes when jurors refuse to find a murderer guilty; when Judges will not sentence him to death, or will recommend him to mercy; or when, if juries and Judges do not flinch from their duty, Home Secretaries, under pressure of deputations and memorials, shrink from theirs, and the threat becomes, as it became in the other cases, a mere *brutum fulmen*; then, indeed, it may become necessary to do in this case what has been done in those—to abrogate the penalty. That time may come—my hon. Friend thinks that it has nearly come. I hardly know whether he lamented it or boasted of it; but he and his Friends are entitled to the boast: for if it comes it will be their doing, and they will have gained what I cannot but call a fatal victory, for they will have achieved it by bringing about, if they will forgive me for saying so, an enervation, an effeminacy, in the general mind of the country. For what else than effeminacy is it to be so much more shocked by taking a man's life then by depriving him of all that makes life desirable or valuable? Is death, then, the greatest of all earthly ills? *Usque adeone mori miserum est?* [Is it, indeed, so dreadful a thing to die?] Has it not been from of old one chief part of a manly education to make us despise death—teaching us to account it, if an evil at all, by no means high in the list of evils; at all events, as an inevitable one,

31

and to hold, as it were, our lives in our hands, ready to be given or risked at any moment, for a sufficiently worthy object? I am sure that my hon. Friends know all this as well, and have as much of all these feelings as any of the rest of us; possibly more. But I cannot think that this is likely to be the effect of their teaching on the general mind.

The Value of Human Life

I cannot think that the cultivating of a peculiar sensitiveness of conscience on this one point, over and above what result from the general cultivation of the moral sentiments, is permanently consistent with assigning in our own minds to the fact of death no more than the degree of relative importance which belongs to it among the other incidents of our humanity. The men of old cared too little about death, and gave their own lives or took those of others with equal recklessness. Our danger is of the opposite kind, lest we should be so much shocked by death, in general and in the abstract, as to care too much about it in individual cases, both those of other people and our own, which call for its being risked. And I am not putting things at the worst, for it is proved by the experience of other countries that horror of the executioner by no means necessarily implies horror of the assassin. The stronghold, as we all know, of hired assassination in the 18th century was Italy; yet it is said that in some of the Italian populations the infliction of death by sentence of law was in the highest degree offensive and revolting to popular feeling. Much has been said of the sanctity of human life, and the absurdity of supposing that we can teach respect for life by ourselves destroying it. But I am surprised at the employment of this argument, for it is one which might be brought against any punishment whatever. It is not human life only, not human life as such, that ought to be sacred to us, but human feelings. The human capacity of suffering is what we should cause to be respected, not the mere capacity of existing. And we may imagine somebody asking how we can teach people not to inflict suffering by ourselves inflicting it? But to this I should answer—all of us would answer—that to deter by suffering from inflicting suffering is not only possible, but the very purpose of penal justice. Does fining a criminal show want of respect for property, or imprisoning him, for personal freedom? Just as unreasonable is it to think that to take the life of a man who has taken that of another is to show want of regard for human life. We show, on the contrary, most emphatically our regard for it, by the adoption of a rule that he who violates that right in another forfeits it for himself, and that while no other crime that he can commit deprives him of his right to live, this shall.

There is one argument against capital punishment, even in ex-

treme cases, which I cannot deny to have weight. . . . It is this—
that if by an error of justice an innocent person is put to death,
the mistake can never be corrected; all compensation, all reparation for the wrong is impossible. This would be indeed a serious objection if these miserable mistakes—among the most trag-
ical occurrences in the whole round of human affairs—could not
be made extremely rare. The argument is invincible where the
mode of criminal procedure is dangerous to the innocent, or
where the Courts of Justice are not trusted. And this probably is
the reason why the objection to an irreparable punishment began (as I believe it did) earlier, and is more intense and more
widely diffused, in some parts of the Continent of Europe than
it is here. There are on the continent great and enlightened
countries, in which the criminal procedure is not so favourable
to innocence, does not afford the same security against erro-
neous conviction, as it does among us; countries where the
Courts of Justice seem to think they fail in their duty unless
they find somebody guilty; and in their really laudable desire to
hunt guilt from its hiding places, expose themselves to a serious
danger of condemning the innocent. If our own procedure and
Courts of Justice afforded ground for similar apprehension, I
should be the first to join in withdrawing the power of inflicting
irreparable punishment from such tribunals. But we all know
that the defects of our procedure are the very opposite.

Perish the Murderers

It is better that the murderer should perish than that innocent men
and women should have their throats cut. A witty Frenchman
lately wrote a pamphlet on this subject, and said—

"I am all for abolishing the penalty of death, if Messieurs the
Assassins would only set the example."

Mr. Gregory, from debate before England's Parliament, April 21, 1868.

Our rules of evidence are even too favourable to the prisoner:
and juries and Judges carry out the maxim, "It is better that ten
guilty should escape than that one innocent person should suffer," not only to the letter, but beyond the letter. Judges are
most anxious to point out, and juries to allow for, the barest possibility of the prisoner's innocence. No human judgment is in-
fallible: such sad cases as my hon. Friend cited will sometimes
occur; but in so grave a case as that of murder, the accused, in
our system, has always the benefit of the merest shadow of a
doubt. And this suggests another consideration very germane to
the question. The very fact that death punishment is more

shocking than any other to the imagination, necessarily renders the courts of Justice more scrupulous in requiring the fullest evidence of guilt. Even that which is the greatest objection to capital punishment, the impossibility of correcting an error once committed, must make, and does make, juries and Judges more careful in forming their opinion, and more jealous in their scrutiny of the evidence.

If the substitution of penal servitude for death in cases of murder should cause any relaxation in this conscientious scrupulosity, there would be a great evil to set against the real, but I hope rare, advantage of being able to make reparation to a condemned person who was afterwards discovered to be innocent. In order that the possibility of correction may be kept open wherever the chance of this sad contingency is more than infinitesimal, it is quite right that the Judge should recommend to the Crown a commutation of the sentence, not solely when the proof of guilt is open to the smallest suspicion, but whenever there remains anything unexplained and mysterious in the case, raising a desire for more light, or making it likely that further information may at some future time be obtained.

Against Total Abolition

I would also suggest that whenever the sentence is commuted the grounds of the commutation should, in some authentic form, be made known to the public. Thus much I willingly concede to my hon. Friend; but on the question of total abolition I am inclined to hope that the feeling of the country is not with him, and that the limitation of death punishment to the cases referred to in the Bill of last year will be generally considered sufficient. The mania which existed a short time ago for paring down all our punishments seems to have reached its limits, and not before it was time. We were in danger of being left without any effectual punishment, except for small offences. . . .

I think . . . that in the case of most offences, except those against property, there is more need of strengthening our punishments than of weakening them: and that severer sentences, with an apportionment of them to the different kinds of offences which shall approve itself better than at present to the moral sentiments of the community, are the kind of reform of which our penal system now stands in need.

"Putting men to death in cold blood by human law . . . seems to me a most pernicious and brutalizing practice."

The Death Penalty Is State-Sanctioned Murder (1872)

Horace Greeley

Horace Greeley is a true American success story. Having grown up in abject poverty and with little education, Greeley founded the *New York Tribune* in 1841 and made it one of the most influential papers in the country. A social reformer, Greeley advocated temperance, women's rights, and a homestead law. In the following viewpoint Greeley addresses four points he believes prove the death penalty is dangerous and brutal.

As you read, consider the following questions:

1. Why does the author argue the death penalty is now obsolete?
2. Why does Greeley believe the death penalty sanctions revenge?

Horace Greeley, *Hints Toward Reforms in Lectures, Addresses, and Other Writings.* New York: Harper & Brothers, 1850.

Is it ever justifiable . . . to [kill] malefactors by sentence of law? I answer Yes, *provided* Society can in no other way be secured against a repetition of the culprit's offence. In committing a murder, for instance, he has proved himself capable of committing more murders—perhaps many. The possibility of a thousand murders is developed in his one act of felonious homicide. Call his moral state depravity, insanity, or whatever you please, he is manifestly a ferocious, dangerous animal, who can not safely be permitted to go at large. Society must be secured against the reasonable probability of his killing others, and, where that can only be effected by taking his life, his life must be taken.

—But suppose him to be in New-England, New-York or Pennsylvania—arrested, secured and convicted—Society's rebel, outcast and prisoner of war—taken with arms in his hands. Here are prison-cells wherefrom escape is impossible; and if there be any fear of his assaulting his keeper or others, that may be most effectively prevented. Is it expedient or salutary to crush the life out of this helpless, abject, pitiable wretch?

A Sorrowful Mistake

I for one think it decidedly *is not*—that it is a sorrowful mistake and barbarity to do any such thing. In saying this, I do not assume to decide whether Hanging or Imprisonment for Life is the severer penalty. I should wish to understand clearly the moral state of the prisoner before I attempted to guess; and, even then, I know too little of the scenes of untried being which lie next beyond the confines of this mortal existence to say whether it were better for any penitent or hardened culprit to be hung next month or left in prison to die a natural death. What is best for that culprit I leave to God, who knows when is the fit time for him to die. My concern is with Society—the moral it teaches, the conduct it tacitly enjoins. And I feel that the choking to death of this culprit works harm, in these respects, namely:

1. *It teaches and sanctions Revenge.* There is a natural inclination in man to return injury for injury, evil for evil. It is the exciting cause of many murders as well as less flagrant crimes. It stands in no need of stimulation—its prompt repression at all times is one of the chief trials even of good men. But A.B. has committed a murder, is convicted of and finally hung for it. Bill, Dick and Jim, three apprentices of ordinary understanding and attainments, beg away or run away to witness the hanging. Ask either of them, 'What is this man hung for?' and the prompt, correct answer will be, 'Because he killed C.D.'—not 'To prevent his killing others,' nor yet 'To prevent others from killing.' Well: the three enjoy the spectacle and turn away satisfied. On their way home, a scuffle is commenced in fun, but gradually

changes to a fight, wherein one finds himself down with two holding and beating him. Though sorely exasperated and severely suffering, he can not throw them off, but he can reach with one hand the knife in his vest pocket. Do you fancy he will be more or less likely to use it because of that moral spectacle which Society has just proffered for his delectation and improvement? You may say Less if you can, but I say More! many times more! You may preach to him that Revenge is right for Society but wrong for him till your head is gray, and he perhaps may listen to you—but not till after he has opened his knife and made a lunge with it.

Death Penalty Unnecessary

It is not necessary to hang the murderer in order to guard society against him, and to prevent him from repeating the crime. If it were, we should hang the maniac, who is the most dangerous murderer. Society may defend itself by other means than by destroying life. Massachusetts can build prisons strong enough to secure the community forever against convicted felons.

Robert Rantoul Jr., *Report to the Legislature*, 1836.

2. *It tends to weaken and destroy the natural horror of bloodshed.* Man has a natural horror of taking the life of his fellow man. His instincts revolt at it—his conscience condemns it—his frame shudders at the thought of it. But let him see first one and then another strung up between heaven and earth and choked to death, with due formalities of Law and solemnities of Religion—the slayer not accounted an evil-doer but an executor of the State's just decree, a pillar of the Social edifice—and his horror of bloodshed *per se* sensibly and rapidly oozes away, and he comes to look at killing men as quite the thing provided there be adequate reason for it. But what reason? and whose? The law slays the slayer; but in his sight the corrupter or calumniator of his wife or sister, the traducer of his character, the fraudulent bankrupt who has involved and ruined his friend, is every whit as great a villian as the man-slayer, and deserving of as severe a punishment. Yet the Law makes no provision for such punishment—hardly for any punishment at all—and what shall he do? He can not consent that the guilty go 'unwhipt of justice,' so he takes his rifle and deals out full measure of it. He is but doing as Society has taught him by example. War, dueling, bloody affrayo, &c., find their nourishment and support in the Gallows.

3. *It facilitates and often insures the escape of the guilty from any punishment by human law.*—Jurors (whether for or against Capital

37

Punishment) dread to convict where the crime is Death. Human judgment is fallible; human testimony may mislead. Witnesses often lie—sometimes conspire to lie plausibly and effectively. Circumstances often strongly point to a conclusion which is after all a false one. The real murderers sometimes conspire to fasten suspicion on some innocent person, and so arrange the circumstances that he can hardly escape their toils. Sometimes they appear in court as witnesses against him, and swear the crime directly upon him. A single legal work contains a list of one hundred cases in which men were hung for crimes which they were afterward proved entirely innocent of. And for every such case there have doubtless been many wherein juries, unwilling to take life where there was a *possibility* of innocence, have given the prisoner the benefit of a very faint doubt and acquitted him. Had the penalty been Imprisonment, they would have convicted, notwithstanding the bare possibility of his innocence, since any future developments in his favor, through the retraction of witnesses, the clearing up of circumstances, or the confession of the actual culprit, would at once lead to his liberation and to an earnest effort by the community to repay him for his unmerited ignominy and suffering. But choke the prisoner to death, and any development in his favor is thenceforth too late. Next year may prove him innocent beyond cavil nor doubt; but of what avail is that to the victim over whose grave the young grass is growing? And thus, through the inexorable character of the Death-Penalty, hundreds of the innocent suffer an undeserved and ignominious death, while tens of thousands of the guilty escape any punishment by human law.

Sympathizing with the Criminal

4. *It excites a pernicious sympathy for the convict.*—We ought ever to be merciful toward the sinful and guilty, remembering our own misdeeds and imperfections. We ought to regard with a benignant compassion those whom Crime has doomed to suffer. But the criminal is not a hero, nor a martyr, and should not be made to resemble one. A crowd of ten to fifty thousand persons, witnessing the infliction of the law's just penalty on an offender, and half of them sobbing and crying from sympathy for his fate, is not a wholesome spectacle—far otherwise. The impression it makes is not that of the majesty and Divine benignity of Law—the sovereignty and beneficence of Justice. Thousands are hoping, praying, entreating that a pardon may yet come— some will accuse the Executive of cruelty and hardness of heart in withholding it. While this furnace of sighs is at red heat, this tempest of sobs in full career, the culprit is swung off—a few faint; many shudder; more feel an acute shock of pain; while the great mass adjourn to take a general drink, some of them

swearing that *this* hanging was a great shame—that the man did not really deserve it. Do you fancy the greater number have imbibed and will profit by the intended lesson?

Capital Punishment

—But I do not care to pile argument on argument, consideration on consideration, in opposition to the expediency, in this day and section, of putting men to death in cold blood by human law. It seems to me a most pernicious and brutalizing practice. Indeed, the recent enactments of our own, with most if not all of the Free States, whereby Executions are henceforth to take place in private, or in the presence of a few select witnesses only, seem clearly to admit the fact. They certainly imply that Executions are of no use as examples—that they rather tend to make criminals than to reform those already depraved. When I see any business or vocation sneaking and skulking in dark lanes and little by-streets which elude observation, I conclude that those who follow such business feel at least doubtful of its utility and beneficence. They may *argue* that it is 'a necessary evil,' but they can hardly put faith in their own logic. When I see the bright array of many-colored liquor bottles, which formerly filled flauntingly the post of honor in every tip-top hotel, now hustled away into some sideroom, and finally down into a dark basement, out of the sight and knowledge of all but those who especially seek them, I say exultingly, 'Good for so much! one more 'hoist, and they will be—where they should be—out of sight 'and reach altogether:'—so, when I see the Gallows, once the denizen of some swelling eminence, the cynosure of ten thousand eyes, 'the observed of all observers,' skulking and hiding itself from public view in jail-yards, shutting itself up in prisons, I say, 'You have taken the right road! Go 'ahead! One more drive, and your detested, rickety frame 'is out of the sight of civilized man for ever!'

"It is the finality of the death penalty which instils fear into the heart of every murderer, and it is this fear of punishment which protects society."

Capital Punishment Is a Safeguard for Society (1925)

Robert E. Crowe

In early 1925, when Judge Robert E. Crowe wrote his opinion of the death penalty, he was state's attorney for Cook County, Illinois. He had just been the prosecutor in the widely publicized trial of Nathan Leopold and Richard Loeb, two young men who were charged with the murder of a young boy. The first World War had not been over for long and America was beginning to focus again on its own growing problem of crime. In this viewpoint Crowe defends the American legal system and the necessity of ridding society of murderers in order to secure safety for its members and deter further murders.

As you read, consider the following questions:

1. Why does the author believe that a murderer is a danger to all of society?
2. How does Crowe think the American system protects the accused criminal?
3. What arguments does the author offer for his statement that capital punishment is a deterrent to crime?

Robert E. Crowe, "Capital Punishment Protects Society," *The Forum*, February 1925.

I believe that the penalty for murder should be death. I urge capital punishment for murder not because I believe that society wishes to take the life of a murderer but because society does not wish to lose its own. I advocate this extreme and irrevocable penalty because the punishment is commensurate with the crime. The records, I believe, will show that the certainty of punishment is a deterrent of crime. As the law is written in most of the States of the Union, every other form of punishment is revocable at the will of an individual.

It is the finality of the death penalty which instils fear into the heart of every murderer, and it is this fear of punishment which protects society. Murderers are not punished for revenge. The man with the life blood of another upon his hands is a menace to the life of every citizen. He should be removed from society for the sake of society. In his removal, society is sufficiently protected, but only provided it is a permanent removal. I should like to see the experiment of the inexorable infliction of the death penalty upon all deliberate murderers tried out in every State of the Union for a sufficient period of time to demonstrate whether or not it is the most effective and most certain means of checking the appalling slaughter of innocent, peaceful, and law-abiding citizens which has gone on without check for so many years, and which is increasing at a rate which has won for the United States of America the disgrace of being known as "the most lawless nation claiming place among the civilized nations of the world."

Duty to Society

The attitude which society must take toward offenders—great as well as small—must not be confused with the attitude which the individual quite properly may assume. Neither may officers of the law nor leaders of public thought, if they are mindful of the duty which they owe to society, advocate a substitution of any other penalty for murder than that penalty which will give to society the greatest degree of protection. . . .

In cases where—in a properly constituted court over whose deliberations a properly elected or appointed judge has presided and in which, after hours and days and sometimes weeks of patient and deliberate inquiry, a jury of twelve men selected in the manner which the law provides—a man charged with murder has been found guilty and sentenced to death, it is an unpardonable abuse of the great power of executive clemency to nullify the verdict by commuting the sentence to life imprisonment. It is in effect a usurpation by the executive authority of the state of powers and duties deliberately and expressly assigned by the representatives of the people in the constitution to the judicial branch alone.

I do not believe that the American Bar is ready to plead guilty to the charge which this action infers that lawyers for the prosecution and lawyers for the defense are so venal, corrupt, and bloodthirsty through ulterior motives as to deliberately conspire with an unrighteous judge, an unprincipled or irresponsible jury and witnesses prompted solely by the spirit of revenge to doom to death any man on a charge of murder unless the testimony truly shows him guilty beyond all reasonable doubt. . . .

Faith in Americans

It is because of my faith and trust in the integrity of our American citizens that I believe that there is no considerable danger that the innocent man will be convicted and that society may be charged that in a blind zeal to protect itself against murder it actually commits murder by the infliction of the death penalty.

The man who kills is society's greatest enemy. He has set up his own law. He is an anarchist—the foe of all civilized government. If anarchy is not to be met with anarchy, it must be met by the laws, and these laws must be enforced. . . .

Penalize Offenders

If we want order, we must stop being soft-headed sentimentalists when it comes to penalizing offenders. The murder rate in the United States rises to a scandalous figure. Of the many who kill, comparatively few are ever arrested, still fewer convicted, fewer yet ever see the inside of a felon's cell; only rarely is the murderer punished as the law says he shall be. A life term is commonly a short vacation at State expense with nothing to do but eat the fruit of others' industry. Americans are not a nation of murder lovers. We merely seem to be. We are made to seem to be by ill-prepared judges, woozy jurors, and a public opinion sentimentally inclined to sympathize more with the perpetrators than the victims of major crimes. This country needs a rededication to the everlasting truth that the fear of prompt and adequate punishment is the best deterrent for gentlemen tempted to slay. This violates long book-shelves of theory.

Cleveland Plain Dealer, January 25, 1925.

Why are there so few violations of the laws of the United States? When a man files his income tax schedule, why does he hire an auditor to see that he makes no mistake, and why does the same man when he goes before our Boards of Assessors and Boards of Review and schedules his personal property for taxation in Chicago as well as elsewhere conceal millions upon which he should be taxed? Why? Because when you get into the United States court after having violated the laws of the United States, if you are guilty, no plea of mercy, however eloquent or

43

by whomsoever delivered, will cheat the law there.

We hear much about England. There murder is murder. Justice is swift and sure. There are fewer murders in the entire Kingdom of Great Britain yearly than there are in the city of Chicago.

In recent years the American public has been influenced to some extent by an active, persistent, and systematic agitation based upon an unfortunate and misplaced sympathy for persons accused of crime. I say unfortunate and misplaced sympathy because it is a sympathy guided by emotion and impulse rather than upon reason and compassion for the prisoners at the bar. It is so deep and soul stirring that it loses its sense of proportion. It forgets the life that was blotted out. It forgets the broken-hearted left behind. It forgets the fatherless and sometimes homeless children which should be the real object of pity. It forgets that they become charges upon the state and it also forgets that there has been established a broken home—the one in the group of homes from which twice as many criminals come as from those which remain intact.

Opponents of capital punishment think somewhat along the same lines. They forget that murder is inexorable and that the victim never returns. They forget that society is protected best by punishment which is proportionate to the crime. They are moved to abolish hanging because it is an unwholesome spectacle. They overlook the unwholesome and harrowing aspects of a murder scene.

Some who admit the justice of capital punishment deny its necessity. They argue that in taking the life of an offender society is wreaking vengeance upon a helpless individual, while, as a matter of fact, the exact opposite is true. If an individual were to slay another who was guilty of murder, especially if he had no fear of him, the act would be prompted by revenge. And when we realize that many of our present-day murderers are professional criminals whose victims were slain in the course of holdups, robberies, and other crimes committed for profit, and that the victim was killed deliberately on the theory that dead men can make no identifications, we know at once that they did not kill for revenge and that they had no malice against the individual they killed. Society for its own protection should make it impossible for these men to kill again.

Crime Against Society

Murder like all other crime is a crime against society. It is for assault upon society that the state inflicts punishment. Too many confuse the relation of the victim of a crime with that of the interest of the state in the prosecution of criminals. The state is impersonal. It is the voice for all of the people expressed by a voting majority. What happens or has happened to any individual is not of great importance. The civil courts exist for the

44

adjudication of the individual and personal wrong. The criminal court exists to punish those who have offended against the state. He who violates the criminal code offends against and injures us all. When he injures to the extent of unlawfully taking human life, he has committed a grave and irreparable injury.

Punishment of the slayer will not bring back life to the victim. But punishment for crime is not inflicted upon any theory of relationship to the victim except to consider the fact that the victim was a part of society and that in wronging the individual that society itself has been assaulted.

Responsibility for Actions

I am not ready to agree to the theory that all or most murderers are not responsible for their acts. I believe that man is entitled to free will and that except in rare instances he is both morally and legally responsible for all his acts. I cannot accept the theory that murderers should not be punished for their crime because they are irresponsible. If they are so irresponsible as to constitute a danger to society, I do not believe that society can carefully preserve in existence the danger they represent. I believe that society is justified in destroying even the irresponsible murderer if he is known to imperil the life of other persons. There should be no sentiment about it. Persons whose existence means death and disaster to others who have done no wrong have no claim upon society for anything—not even for life itself.

Safety of Citizens

Nothing is more remarkable in the evolution of a community than the growing regard for human life. A community is held to be civilized, or not, in exact proportion to the safety of the common citizen. When the life of an individual is unjustly taken by another individual, the horror of the community for such an act cannot be adequately and proportionately manifested except as the community surmounts sentiment and exacts the life of the killer in payment—after a trial, where all opportunity of defense is accorded, and after all possible human excuses and palliations have been alleged, tested, and found insufficient.

R. L. Calder, "Is Capital Punishment Right? A Debate," *The Forum*, September 1928.

Few men who murder have previously lived blameless lives. The act of murder is the climax—a cumulative effect of countless previous thoughts and acts. The man's conduct depends upon his philosophy of life. Those who want to grow up to be respectable and useful citizens in the community have a correct philosophy. Those who want to excel in crime, those who tear down instead of building up, deliberately choose to adopt the wrong philosophy of life and to make their conduct correspond with it.

Society and particularly the state would not be much concerned with individual codes of conduct if, at the present time, they were not adopted by the youths of the land and were not creating an army of virtual anarchists who look upon the criminal code, including that part of it forbidding murder, as a mere convention of society which "advanced thinking" and crazy social theories permit them to set aside as a matter of no consequence.

Because some of the youth of our population are saturated with these ideas, we are asked to accept fantastic notions, abnormal actions, and even defiance, disregard, and violation of the law, as the reason for turning them loose when charged with murder. We are compelled to listen to the weirdest, wildest, and most fantastic theories expounded by expert witnesses to show why capital punishment should not be inflicted. . . .

If the United States of America has the power to take boys of eighteen years of age and send them to their death in the front line trenches in countries overseas in defense of our laws, I believe that the state has an equal right to take the lives of murderers of like age for violating the mandate of God and man, "Thou shalt not kill."

Deterrent of Crime

I base my belief that capital punishment is a deterrent of crime upon the fact that where capital punishment has been inflicted for even a comparatively small period and in a relatively small number of cases, there subsequently has been an immediate decrease in murder. Those who argue against capital punishment should bear in mind that where capital punishment has actually been inflicted, this has been the result. But, capital punishment has never been given a fair trial throughout this country over a sufficient period of time and in a sufficient number of cases to justify the assumption that it is not a deterrent of murder.

Until American society finds a way to protect itself from the murder of its members, this country will continue to be known as "the most lawless nation claiming place among the civilized nations of the world." I am not proud of that appellation. I hang my head in shame whenever I hear it. I believe society should have no hesitancy in springing the trap every time the noose can be put around a murderer's neck.

"It is hardly probable that the great majority of people refrain from killing their neighbors because they are afraid; they refrain because they never had the inclination."

Capital Punishment Will Not Safeguard Society (1928)

Clarence Darrow

Clarence Darrow was a Chicago lawyer who became famous for his handling of criminal and labor cases. He chose to defend those whom he considered social unfortunates. He argued on behalf of more than one hundred people charged with murder, none of whom were sentenced to death. Although he retired in 1927, he continued to write prolifically on the causes of crime and to argue vehemently for the abolition of the death penalty. His most famous courtroom pleas are included in the book *Attorney for the Damned.* In the following viewpoint, Darrow maintains that capital punishment is no deterrent to crime. He advances his theory that as victims of their culture, criminals need to be treated more humanely.

As you read, consider the following questions:

1. To what does Darrow attribute the causes of crime, specifically murder?
2. What arguments does the author offer to support his belief that capital punishment is no deterrent to murder?

Clarence Darrow, "The Futility of the Death Penalty," *The Forum*, September 1928.

Little more than a century ago, in England, there were over two hundred offenses that were punishable with death. The death sentence was passed upon children under ten years old. And every time the sentimentalist sought to lessen the number of crimes punishable by death, the self-righteous said no, that it would be the destruction of the state; that it would be better to kill for more transgressions rather than for less.

Today, both in England and America, the number of capital offenses has been reduced to a very few, and capital punishment would doubtless be abolished altogether were it not for the self-righteous, who still defend it with the same old arguments. Their major claim is that capital punishment decreases the number of murders, and hence, that the state must retain the institution as its last defense against the criminal.

It is my purpose in this article to prove, first, that capital punishment is no deterrent to crime; and second, that the state continues to kill its victims, not so much to defend society against them—for it could do that equally well by imprisonment—but to appease the mob's emotions of hatred and revenge.

The Criminal Disease

Behind the idea of capital punishment lies false training and crude views of human conduct. People do evil things, say the judges, lawyers, and preachers, because of depraved hearts. Human conduct is not determined by the causes which determine the conduct of other animal and plant life in the universe. For some mysterious reason human beings act as they please; and if they do not please to act in a certain way, it is because, having the power of choice, they deliberately choose to act wrongly. The world once applied this doctrine to disease and insanity in men. It was also applied to animals, and even inanimate things were once tried and condemned to destruction. The world knows better now, but the rule has not yet been extended to human beings.

The simple fact is that every person starts life with a certain physical structure, more or less sensitive, stronger or weaker. He is played upon by everything that reaches him from without, and in this he is like everything else in the universe, inorganic matter as well as organic. How a man will act depends upon the character of his human machine, and the strength of the various stimuli that affect it. Everyone knows that this is so in disease and insanity. Most investigators know that it applies to crime. But the great mass of people still sit in judgment, robed with self-righteousness, and determine the fate of their less fortunate fellows. When this question is studied like any other, we shall then know how to get rid of most of the conduct that we call "criminal," just as we are now getting rid of much of the disease that once afflicted mankind.

If crime were really the result of willful depravity, we should be ready to concede that capital punishment may serve as a deterrent to the criminally inclined. But it is hardly probable that the great majority of people refrain from killing their neighbors because they are afraid; they refrain because they never had the inclination. Human beings are creatures of habit and, as a rule, they are not in the habit of killing. The circumstances that lead to killings are manifold, but in a particular individual the inducing cause is not easily found. In one case, homicide may have been induced by indigestion in the killer; in another, it may be traceable to some weakness inherited from a remote ancestor; but that it results from *something* tangible and understandable, if all the facts were known, must be plain to everyone who believes in cause and effect.

Punishment No Cure for Crime

There is no deterrent in the menace of the gallows.

Cruelty and viciousness are not abolished by cruelty and viciousness—not even by legalized cruelty and viciousness. . . .

Our penal system has broken down because it is built upon the sand—founded on the basis of force and violence—instead of on the basis of Christian care of our fellow men, of moral and mental human development, of the conscientious performance by the State of its duty to the citizen.

We cannot cure murder by murder.

We must adopt another and better system.

William Randolph Hearst, *The Congressional Digest*, August/September 1927.

Of course, no one will be converted to this point of view by statistics of crime. In the first place, it is impossible to obtain reliable ones; and in the second place, the conditions to which they apply are never the same. But if one cares to analyze the figures, such as we have, it is easy to trace the more frequent causes of homicide. The greatest number of killings occur during attempted burglaries and robberies. The robber knows that penalties for burglary do not average more than five years in prison. He also knows that the penalty for murder is death or life imprisonment. Faced with this alternative, what does the burglar do when he is detected and threatened with arrest? He shoots to kill. He deliberately takes the chance of death to save himself from a five-year term in prison. It is therefore as obvious as anything can be that fear of death has no effect in diminishing homicides of this kind, which are more numerous than any other type.

The next largest number of homicides may be classed as "sex murders." Quarrels between husbands and wives, disappointed love, or love too much requited cause many killings. They are the result of primal emotions so deep that the fear of death has not the slightest effect in preventing them. Spontaneous feelings overflow in criminal acts, and consequences do not count. Then there are cases of sudden anger, uncontrollable rage. The fear of death never enters into such cases; if the anger is strong enough, consequences are not considered until too late. The old-fashioned stories of men deliberately plotting and committing murder in cold blood have little foundation in real life. Such killings are so rare that they need not concern us here. The point to be emphasized is that practically all homicides are manifestations of well-recognized human emotions, and it is perfectly plain that the fear of excessive punishment does not enter into them.

In addition to these personal forces which overwhelm weak men and lead them to commit murder, there are also many social and economic forces which must be listed among the causes of homicides, and human beings have even less control over these than over their own emotions. It is often said that in America there are more homicides in proportion to population than in England. This is true. There are likewise more in the United States than in Canada. But such comparisons are meaningless until one takes into consideration the social and economic differences in the countries compared. Then it becomes apparent why the homicide rate in the United States is higher. Canada's population is largely rural; that of the United States is crowded into cities whose slums are the natural breeding places of crime. Moreover, the population of England and Canada is homogeneous, while the United States has gathered together people of every color from every nation in the world. Racial differences intensify social, religious, and industrial problems, and the confusion which attends this indiscriminate mixing of races and nationalities is one of the most fertile sources of crime.

Primitive Beliefs

Will capital punishment remedy these conditions? Of course it won't; but its advocates argue that the fear of this extreme penalty will hold the victims of adverse conditions in check. To this piece of sophistry the continuance and increase of crime in our large cities is a sufficient answer. No, the plea that capital punishment acts as a deterrent to crime will not stand. The real reason why this barbarous practice persists in a so-called civilized world is that people still hold the primitive belief that the taking of one human life can be atoned for by taking another. It is the age-old obsession with punishment that keeps the official headsman busy plying his trade.

And it is precisely upon this point that I would build my case against capital punishment. Even if one grants that the idea of punishment is sound, crime calls for something more—for careful study, for an understanding of causes, for proper remedies. To attempt to abolish crime by killing the criminal is the easy and foolish way out of a serious situation. Unless a remedy deals with the conditions which foster crime, criminals will breed faster than the hangman can spring his trap. Capital punishment ignores the causes of crime just as completely as the primitive witch doctor ignored the causes of disease; and, like the methods of the witch doctor, it is not only ineffective as a remedy, but is positively vicious in at least two ways. In the first place, the spectacle of state executions feeds the basest passions of the mob. And in the second place, so long as the state rests content to deal with crime in this barbaric and futile manner, society will be lulled by a false sense of security, and effective methods of dealing with crime will be discouraged. . . .

Crime in England

For the last five or six years, in England and Wales, the homicides reported by the police range from sixty-five to seventy a year. Death sentences meted out by jurors have averaged about thirty-five, and hangings, fifteen. More than half of those convicted by juries were saved by appeals to the Home Office. But in America there is no such percentage of lives saved after conviction. Governors are afraid to grant clemency. If they did, the newspapers and the populace would refuse to reelect them.

Failure to Instill Fear

It is a fact that a large percentage of murders are committed in the heat of passion, when the murderer is not in a position to reason; fear of the law plays no part at all. In the remaining few, whatever fear there may be is more than balanced by the belief on the part of the criminal that he is not going to get caught. There are also some who deliberately kill; but the knowledge that they will be caught and punished does not deter them.

Thomas Mott Osborne, "Thou Shalt Not Kill," *The Forum*, February 1925.

It is true that trials are somewhat prompter in England than America, but there no newspaper dares publish the details of any case until after the trial. In America the accused is often convicted by the public within twenty-four hours of the time a homicide occurs. The courts sidetrack all other business so that a homicide that is widely discussed may receive prompt attention. The road to the gallows is not only opened but greased for the opportunity of killing another victim. . . .

Human conduct is by no means so simple as our moralists have led us to believe. There is no sharp line separating good actions from bad. The greed for money, the display of wealth, the despair of those who witness the display, the poverty, oppression, and hopelessness of the unfortunate—all these are factors which enter into human conduct and of which the world takes no account. Many people have learned no other profession but robbery and burglary. The processions moving steadily through our prisons to the gallows are in the main made up of these unfortunates. And how do we dare to consider ourselves civilized creatures when, ignoring the causes of crime, we rest content to mete our harsh punishments to the victims of conditions over which they have no control?

Even now, are not all imaginative and humane people shocked at the spectacle of a killing by the state? How many men and women would be willing to act as executioners? How many fathers and mothers would want their children to witness an official killing? What kind of people read the sensational reports of an execution? If all right-thinking men and women were not ashamed of it, why would it be needful that judges and lawyers and preachers apologize for the barbarity? How can the state censure the cruelty of the man who—moved by strong passions, or acting to save his freedom, or influenced by weakness or fear—takes human life, when everyone knows that the state itself, after long premeditation and settled hatred, not only kills, but first tortures and bedevils its victims for weeks with the impending doom?

More Humane Criminal Code

For the last hundred years the world has shown a gradual tendency to mitigate punishment. We are slowly learning that this way of controlling human beings is both cruel and ineffective. In England the criminal code has consistently grown more humane, until now the offenses punishable by death are reduced to practically one. If there is any reason for singling out this one, neither facts nor philosophy can possibly demonstrate it. There is no doubt whatever that the world is growing more humane and more sensitive and more understanding. The time will come when all people will view with horror the light way in which society and its courts of law now take human life; and when that time comes, the way will be clear to devise some better method of dealing with poverty and ignorance and their frequent by-products which we call crime.

Evaluating Sources of Information

When historians study and interpret past events, they use two kinds of sources: primary and secondary. Primary sources are eyewitness accounts. For example, the diary of a prisoner on death row would be a primary source. A study of death row prisoners that quotes from the diary is an example of a secondary source. Primary and secondary sources may be decades or even hundreds of years old, and often historians find that the sources offer conflicting and contradictory information. To fully evaluate documents and assess their accuracy, historians analyze the credibility of the documents' authors and, in the case of secondary sources, analyze the credibility of the information the authors used.

Historians are not the only people who encounter conflicting information, however. Anyone who reads a daily newspaper, watches television, or just talks to different people will encounter many different views. Writers and speakers use sources of information to support their own statements. Thus, critical thinkers, just like historians, must question the writer's or speaker's sources of information as well as the writer or speaker.

While there are many criteria that can be applied to assess the accuracy of a primary or secondary source, for this activity you will be asked to apply three. For each source listed on the following page, ask yourself the following questions: First, did the person actually see or participate in the event he or she is reporting? This will help you determine the credibility of the information—an eyewitness to an event is an extremely valuable source. Second, does the person have a vested interest in the report? Assessing the person's social status, professional affiliations, nationality, and religious or political beliefs will be helpful in considering this question. By evaluating this you will be able to determine how objective the person's report may be. Third, how qualified is the author to be making the statements he or she is making? Consider what the person's profession is and how he or she might know about the event. Someone who has spent years being involved with or studying the issue may be able to offer more information than someone who simply is offering an uneducated opinion; for example, a politician or layperson.

Keeping the above criteria in mind, imagine you are writing a paper on the death penalty in America. You decide to cite an equal number of primary and secondary sources. Listed below are several sources which may be useful for your research. *Place a P next to those descriptions you believe are primary sources. Place an S next to those descriptions you believe are secondary sources.* Next, based on the above criteria, *rank the primary sources assigning the number (1) to what appears to be the most valuable, (2) to the source likely to be the second-most valuable, and so on, until all the primary sources are ranked. Then rank the secondary sources, again using the above criteria.*

		Rank in
P or S		*Importance*
_____	1. The courtroom plea of a criminal asking for life imprisonment rather than the death penalty.	_____
_____	2. A study presenting sentencing statistics that determines poor murderers have a greater chance of being sentenced to death.	_____
_____	3. A collection of essays by murder victims' families, expressing why they support or oppose the death penalty.	_____
_____	4. The text from the U.S. Supreme Court's decision in *Furman v. Georgia*, concluding the death penalty is handed down unfairly and arbitrarily.	_____
_____	5. A 1990 book discussing the death penalty in America in the nineteenth century.	_____
_____	6. An anthropologist's study comparing the death penalty practices of ten nations.	_____
_____	7. A defense attorney's closing remarks to a jury that may sentence the attorney's client to death.	_____
_____	8. The text of psychologist James Dobson's interview with serial killer Ted Bundy, just hours before Bundy's execution.	_____
_____	9. An article by James Dobson, summarizing the comments Ted Bundy made during his interview.	_____
_____	10. A historian's 1989 analysis of the 1951 trial and sentencing of Julius and Ethel Rosenberg.	_____

Is the Death Penalty Just?

Chapter Preface

In May 1990, Dalton Prejean was executed in Louisiana for the 1977 murder of a Louisiana state trooper. Awaiting the execution were two women: Candy Cleveland, the wife of murdered state trooper Donald Cleveland, and Helen Prejean (no relation to the executed man), a Sister of St. Joseph and director of Pilgrimage for Life, an anti-death-penalty group. For Candy Cleveland, the execution was the justice for which she had waited thirteen years. For Helen Prejean, it was an unjust murder committed by the state. The dissimilar views of these two women reflect the divisions between those Americans who view the death penalty as a just punishment and those who view it as unjust.

Many Americans, angry and frightened about crimes such as Dalton Prejean's, believe the death penalty is a just punishment for crimes that show a wanton disregard for life. John Scully, attorney for the Washington Legal Foundation, echoes the view of many death penalty supporters when he argues: "There are some crimes so heinous that the death penalty is the only appropriate sentence." Scully and others believe that by requiring murderers to forfeit their lives, society is sending the message that life is valuable and that the price of taking a life is high.

Other Americans, though equally angered by crime, are horrified by the thought of execution. Killing is murder, they argue, whether it is done by a criminal or by the state. Coretta Scott King, wife of slain civil rights leader Martin Luther King Jr., states, "I stand firmly and unequivocally opposed to the death penalty. . . . Justice is never advanced in the taking of human life." King and others believe that a society that values life and justice cannot ethically take the life of any of its citizens.

The issue of fair punishment is an important one to any nation that values justice. The authors in the following chapter debate whether the death sentence is a just penalty for murder.

"By imposing [the death] penalty on those who dare break the most basic rule of existence, we affirm the dignity of every other individual."

The Death Penalty Is Just

Jacob Sullum

Execution is a just penalty for murder, Jacob Sullum argues in the following viewpoint. Sullum believes that by requiring those who take life to forfeit their own lives, society shows that it places a high value on the life of every citizen. Sullum is an assistant editor at *Reason* magazine, a monthly periodical of libertarian social and political thought.

As you read, consider the following questions:

1. Why does Sullum believe that the issue of deterrence is of minor relevance to the debate over the death penalty?
2. How does the author differentiate between revenge and retribution?
3. What does Sullum think is the true mark of civilization?

Jacob Sullum, "Capital Punishment: Yes." Reprinted, with permission, from the June 1990 issue of *Reason* magazine. Copyright © 1990 by the Reason Foundation, 2716 Ocean Park Blvd., Suite 1062, Santa Monica, CA 90405.

Few questions of public policy stir the passions the way the death penalty does. The idea of deliberately taking a human life elicits strong visceral reactions. The vast majority of Americans tend to focus on the act of the murderer and therefore favor capital punishment. A sizable minority, however, concentrates on the act of the state, rejecting it with equal fervor.

Still, those who honestly reflect on the arguments of the other side cannot help but be disconcerted, if not swayed. Although they may return to their original position, they will do so better equipped to distinguish between the crucial and peripheral issues.

Prevention and deterrence, although frequently stressed in news coverage of the death-penalty debate, turn out to be of minor relevance. Capital punishment obviously has some impact on future murders, if only by stopping those who are executed from killing again. But that direct effect could in principle be achieved through lifetime imprisonment without parole.

Deterrence Debate

As for the death penalty's indirect effect on crime, opponents note the dearth of evidence to support the intuitively appealing notion that the prospect of execution discourages potential murderers more than the possibility of a life term would. Advocates respond that deterrence would be stronger if the death penalty were imposed more consistently and carried out more promptly. Since murderers are not very likely to face either execution or life imprisonment, it is difficult to settle this debate.

Moreover, it's unnecessary. In the final analysis, the argument for capital punishment rests on the proposition that in cases of unprovoked, premeditated murder, justice requires it. This assertion is often supported, imprecisely but not inappropriately, through anecdotes intended to provoke moral outrage.

Consider the case of Robert Alton Harris, who was scheduled to be executed by the state of California until he was granted a stay. Harris was convicted in 1979 of kidnapping and murdering two teenagers whose car he stole to commit a bank robbery. The act was cold, callous, and calculated. He killed his victims after telling them they would not be harmed, shooting one as he walked away and the other as he begged for mercy. Afterward, Harris laughed about the murders and finished the boys' lunches.

Does such a man deserve to live? Most people would say no, but they might still question whether the state may therefore take his life. They might ask how the state acquires such a right. They might also argue that even if the government may rightfully execute someone like Harris, it should refrain from doing so because such legally sanctioned killing demeans human life.

One way of responding to the first point is to ask what would happen in a state of nature following a murder. In the case of other crimes, the victim or the victim's agent would have the right to punish the aggressor. Could an offender avoid punishment by killing the victim? Surely not; the right of punishment would pass to relatives or friends of the person who was murdered. If so, they could legitimately transfer that right to an agency, such as the government, that assumes the function of punishing aggressors.

Reprinted by permission: Tribune Media Services.

But should the punishment be death? Isn't this simply revenge? To respond, "No, it is retribution, and therefore just and proper," might seem to be semantic evasion. But what distinguishes revenge from retribution is the motive. The execution of a murderer makes a statement. It says that people like Robert Alton Harris have committed a crime so grave that they have forfeited their right to live; it elevates human life even as it ends the killer's.

Execution of the Innocent

Some people accept this view of the death penalty while retaining pragmatic objections to capital punishment. The most compelling is the fear that an innocent person might be executed. Of course, the possibility of unjust punishment exists with or without the death penalty, and while people who are wrongly imprisoned can be released, nothing can restore the years they have lost. Still, the finality of execution requires that accused murderers be given every reasonable opportunity to challenge their convictions. Stricter limits on appeals are nevertheless appropriate in cases, such as Harris's, where the facts of the crime are not in dispute.

Another practical issue is the inconsistent application of the death penalty. To pick just one notorious example, isn't it unjust to give Hillside Strangler Angelo Buono—who kidnapped, tortured, and murdered nine women—a life sentence, while sending Harris to death row? Yes, but the injustice is not in executing Harris; it's in failing to execute Buono.

Upholding the Right to Life

It is fashionable in some circles to view capital punishment as a barbaric institution that is destined to fade away. Watching some of the macabre pro-death-penalty demonstrations attracted by pending executions, one is tempted to agree. But the true mark of civilization is the extent to which a society upholds the rights of its members, especially the right to life. There is only one appropriate penalty for the willful, unprovoked violation of that right. By imposing this penalty on those who dare to break the most basic rule of existence, we affirm the dignity of every other individual.

"The death penalty always holds the potential for interfering mightily with justice."

The Death Penalty Is Unjust

Lloyd Steffen

Lloyd Steffen is a professor of philosophy and religion at Northland College in Ashland, Wisconsin, and the author of *Self-Deception and the Common Life*. In the following viewpoint, Steffen argues that execution is not a just penalty for any crime. Killing for any reason is immoral, Steffen asserts, and he believes the death penalty is simply state-sanctioned murder.

As you read, consider the following questions:

1. What kinds of people does the author believe are most likely to be executed?
2. Why is Steffen cautious about allowing individual stories of murderers and victims to govern thinking about the death penalty?
3. Why does the author believe James Richardson's case is a challenge to capital punishment?

Lloyd Steffen, "Casting the First Stone," *Christianity and Crisis*, February 5, 1990. Reprinted with permission.

Once again, America has made its peace with capital punishment. Since the moratorium on executions was lifted in 1975, courts and state legislatures have worked hard, and successfully, to reinstate the death penalty. Politically, the issue is no longer even interesting. As the 1988 presidential debates showed, what public debate exists around capital punishment is likely to be about its effectiveness as social policy, not with its status as a *moral* (or even legal) problem. And as social policy opinion polls tell us, America approves of the death penalty. Indeed, it seems to satisfy the American sense of justice and fair play. Given this context, it might seem futile even to ask whether capital punishment can still *be* a moral problem.

Yet even though opponents of capital punishment are in the minority today, they should not allow themselves to be placed on the defensive. A burden of moral proof in the debate over capital punishment still must be borne by those who support it. The death penalty must still be questioned as a moral act because it affronts the moral principle that the deliberate and premeditated taking of fully sentient human life is wrong. Therefore, it falls to those who support it to argue convincingly that killing convicted criminals is morally justifiable and not fundamentally destructive of the moral presumption against such killing.

Failure to debate the moral justifications for capital punishment could well lead to a situation where the practice of executing criminals is simply taken for granted. We may no longer demand a *particular* argument for capital punishment, one that is rationally compelling and able to withstand serious challenges; rather, we may come to assume that such an argument exists—somewhere. We could then justify the death penalty by the kind of moral "intuition" that concludes: "If it were really wrong we would not do it." At that point, capital punishment becomes a noncontroversial issue. . . .

The Innocence of the State

Once a society decides that it is useful to kill people—even people guilty of morally abhorrent acts—sanctity-of-life questions are no longer even arguable, since human life is de facto not sacred. Only those societies or states that have convinced themselves they can act as if they possessed absolute innocence can assume, in good conscience, the power to make premeditated killing a useful means to political and social ends. And, as history shows, when such states or societies acquire the power to decide which acts constitute crimes deserving death, the inevitable criterion is this: those acts that challenge the idea of absolute innocence.

Capital punishment is always potentially an instrument of social repression and political terrorism. As we have seen in China and Iran, when the state claims the power to impose this punishment, it is not the notorious on whom death is most likely to be inflicted, but the nameless and obscure. Even though Americans who support the death penalty can express outrage over the executions that have occurred in these faraway places, the fact is that the 2000 condemned persons currently sitting on America's death rows are also nameless and obscure. The difference is that Americans can apparently justify killing those who disrupt our social order because our social order is "morally superior."

Danziger for *The Christian Science Monitor* © 1990 TCSPS. Reprinted with permission.

The myth of American innocence has suffered greatly in recent years. Yet it persists. Manifest destiny is still alive in the American consciousness. The myth of moral purity continues to affect how we who are not guilty separate ourselves from those who are; and those who are guilty continue to be predominantly poor, male, members of minority groups, now even those with mental disabilities. Are these people so painful a reminder of our national failure that we have deceived ourselves into thinking our innocence can be maintained if they are eliminated? Is capital punishment so popular today because it stands as a symbol of noncomplicity in antisocial acts? Does it serve the national will by perpetuating the illusion of American innocence, which is, after all, our ideological heritage?

My arguments, however, may seem to miss the point. Clearly

the moral passion in support of the death penalty comes not from thinking about capital punishment in abstract ways, but as a just means of retribution for individual crimes perpetrated by individual miscreants on individual victims. Nonetheless, I want to interject a caution. While individual stories certainly activate the moral imagination, dangers always exist in allowing them to govern our thinking about issues that have profound social implications. Individual stories appeal to definite moral principles even if the principles themselves are not articulated, and when we appeal to them rather than to a formal moral argument, we beg questions regarding which principles should be invoked to help us decide that one story rather than another should govern behavior and guide action. Despite these problems, I can still imagine advocates of capital punishment defending their position simply by saying "What about Theodore Bundy?"

An Irrevocable Penalty

Bundy, who died in 1989 in Florida's electric chair, is as strong an anecdotal defense of capital punishment as we could find: A mass murderer who killed innocent women in several states, Bundy appeared to be a moral incorrigible, one who killed repeatedly and without inhibition, and who provided investigators with information about many of his unsolved crimes only because it was the last card he could play to postpone his execution. Seemingly incapable of remorse, Bundy was unquestionably guilty of the crimes for which he had been convicted and many for which he hadn't. If anyone embodies the kind of moral monster who deserves the most severe punishment society can inflict, Ted Bundy did.

But if Ted Bundy's story "argues" for capital punishment, James Richardson's argues even more strongly against it.

In 1968, Richardson, a black Florida fruit picker, was tried and convicted of killing his seven children. Richardson allegedly had taken out insurance policies the night before the murder. While this established motive sufficient to convince a jury of his guilt, neither the defense attorney nor the prosecutor pointed out that the unpaid policies were not in effect when the children died. When Richardson's three cell mates were brought in to testify that he had confessed the crime to them, no one bothered to mention that the sheriff had promised the three reduced jail time for their testimony. The one surviving witness of the three has finally admitted that Richardson never made such a confession. Richardson's lie detector results disappeared and were never disclosed, and the polygraph operator who administered another test to him in prison stated that he had "no involvement in the crime whatsoever."

Richardson's next-door neighbor actually poisoned the children while Richardson and his wife were working in the fields.

Yet she was never called to testify. The authorities did not want the jury to know that her first husband had died mysteriously after eating a dinner she had prepared or that she had actually served four years in prison for killing her second husband. The woman, incidentally, after being admitted to a nursing home, confessed to staff there that she was the guilty party, but the staff, fearing loss of their jobs, did not report her confession to superiors. And the former assistant prosecutor in the town of Arcadia, where Richardson was tried, deliberately concealed over 900 pages of evidence that would have brought all of these facts to light. It took an actual theft to get these documents into the hands of *Miami Herald* reporters. Once there, the case was reopened, and after spending 21 years in prison for a crime he did not commit, James Richardson was released.

Richardson may not have been executed, but his is a story about capital punishment nonetheless. For he was sentenced to death, sat for four years on death row, and was even put through a harrowing "dry run" execution, complete with a shaving and a buckle-down in the chair. Richardson was not only a poor black man who received an inept defense. He was also an innocent man who was made a victim of lies, deceit, perjured testimony, false witnesses—and those who prosecuted him and knew of his innocence still demanded that he be executed. What the Richardson case points out is that the death penalty always holds the potential for interfering mightily with justice. In the Richardson case, guilt lies with the accusers, and the irrevocable nature of the death penalty would have prevented Richardson from receiving even the modicum of justice he finally did receive. Despite being the result of a legal process, his death would have constituted an unjustified killing—an actual murder.

Justice and Social Murder

How is justice to be exacted when a murder is committed by all of society? Is guilt to attach only to the sheriff and prosecutor in the case? Would those two be appropriate targets for the death penalty today since they violated the moral prohibition against the taking of human life and sought deliberately and with premeditation to kill an innocent man—the crime for which we wish to impose death fairly and without caprice? That these events can occur leads to a question: Is killing a Theodore Bundy so necessary that we should accept the risk capital punishment poses to a James Richardson?

Supporters of capital punishment will say justice prevailed; Richardson did not die, and the case poses no challenge. I say, however, that Richardson's case is a fundamental challenge to capital punishment, since the only good thing to come out of the situation is the simple fact that he did not die. His innocence might have come to light even if he had been killed, so it is life,

65

not just truth, that is at stake. Only the simple fact that Richardson is alive makes possible any hope for his seeking restitution from a system that at one point forsook justice and actually conspired to kill him.

No Moral Certainty

If Richardson had been executed and the truth found out, we might not even be asking whether it is morally permissible to continue a practice that by its very nature runs the risk of committing murder and depriving persons of any opportunity to redress injustice. Were Richardson dead, we would be facing social complicity in his death and probably looking for a way to justify his death in order to make it something other than murder. We would be defending ourselves with the very truths we refused to acknowledge to him: that our system of justice is fallible, that our knowledge and judgment can be swayed and distorted, that our moral certainty is neither pure nor absolute.

"Death is a fitting punishment for those who are guilty."

Christians Can Morally Support the Death Penalty

Michael Pakaluk

Michael Pakaluk is a professor of philosophy at Clark University in Worcester, Massachusetts. In the following viewpoint, Pakaluk contends that Christians can and should support the death penalty as a just punishment for murder. He believes the death penalty gives the condemned the chance to pay for the murder and benefits society by ensuring that justice is done.

As you read, consider the following questions:

1. Why did Immanuel Kant oppose life imprisonment, according to Pakaluk?
2. What three factors does the author believe are required for a punishment to be just?
3. What must a society acknowledge before it shows mercy to those condemned to die, in the author's view?

Michael Pakaluk, "Till Death Do Us Part," *Crisis*, September 1989. Reprinted with permission from *Crisis* magazine, PO Box 1006, Notre Dame, IN 46556.

Twenty-eight-year-old Mark Chicano cried out in agony. He had just been sentenced by a panel of Connecticut judges to 260 years in jail—effectively a life sentence—for the murder of three persons. In February of 1987, Chicano had listened outside his girlfriend's bedroom window as she made love with another man. Chicano then broke into her house, and after waiting 40 minutes, he attacked the couple and killed them. When his girlfriend's 11-year-old stepson appeared at the bedroom door, Chicano killed him also.

Chicano lunged at the judges and cried out when the sentence was pronounced, not because of its severity, but because of its leniency. "I must be killed," he shouted, "I must be punished for what I did." Chicano said repeatedly. "I am deeply, deeply sorry. You got to kill me." And then he added an ominous threat: "If you don't put me to death, I will, one way or another." Chicano had to be wrestled to the ground by seven sheriffs before he could be taken out of the courtroom.

The anguish of this man, and his brutal remorse, called to mind Immanuel Kant's famous discussion of capital punishment. Kant argued that life imprisonment was necessarily too mild or too severe a punishment for murder, depending upon the state of mind of the guilty person. If the guilty man is unrepentant, Kant said, then life imprisonment is too mild, since the murderer might enjoy many years of life without any pangs of regret, whereas, if the convict is remorseful, then life imprisonment is too severe, since he is then compelled to live with his sorrow. Kant observed that, by contrast, the death sentence seems adapted to provide the most appropriate punishment in each of the two cases. The repentant convict recognizes that he deserves to die for what he has done, and so the death penalty matches his own judgment; and the unrepentant convict is punished by being deprived of his own life, which he has esteemed even more than doing what is right.

Perhaps Mark Chicano was emotionally disturbed in a manner that partially exculpated him for his crimes, and his outburst at sentencing was a sign of continuing imbalance. Or perhaps Chicano's self-condemnation is sound, and, because no one else will recognize this, he has been driven to a wild frustration. In any case, it is easy to imagine perfectly sane murderers who, like the "man of honor" Kant speaks of, think it fitting that they be put to death for their crimes.

Catholic Views

There are Catholics who believe . . . that "no crime deserves the death penalty." If, for example, they were friends of a guilty criminal on death row, their task, they think, would be to present appeals and press for a commuted sentence, insisting up to the last moment that the death penalty was unjustified, or barbaric, or cruel. They would probably take it for granted that other Catholics should join with them in trying to block the execution. And probably the last thing they would expect, or want, is that their friend should join with those who hold out for the death penalty and say, "Stop what you are doing; I deserve to die for what I did."

An Ethical Imperative

Nowhere does the Bible repudiate capital punishment for premeditated murder; not only is the death penalty for deliberate killing of a fellow-human permitted, but it is approved and encouraged, and for any government that attaches at least as much value to the life of an innocent victim as to a deliberate murderer, it is ethically imperative.

Carl F. H. Henry, *Twilight of a Great Civilization*, 1988.

Yet this attitude—"I deserve to die for my sin"—is a profoundly Christian one. It would seem to be a necessary part of true repentance for having committed any serious sin. After Nathan rebuked David for his adultery and murder of Uriah, David exclaimed, "I have sinned against the Lord," to which Nathan replied, "The Lord also has taken away your sin; you shall not die." Nathan implied that David, in recognizing his sin, recognized also that he deserved the punishment of death. Indeed, if "no crime deserves the death penalty," then it is hard to see why it was fitting that Christ be *put to death* for our sins and crucified among thieves. St. Thomas Aquinas quotes a gloss of St. Jerome on Matthew 27:33: "As Christ became accursed of the cross for us, for our salvation He was crucified as a guilty one among the guilty." That Christ be put to death *as* a guilty person, in place of guilty persons, presupposes that death *is* a fitting punishment for those who are guilty.

Natural Justice

The Church's teaching on capital punishment is sometimes presented in this way: "The state has the right to put those who commit serious crimes to death for the sake of the common good." This is an adequate but misleading statement, insofar as it seems to attribute some special and indeed fearful power to the state—that of putting persons to death. Yet this power no more belongs to the state in itself than the power to legislate belongs to the state in itself. Just as the state's authority to legislate is grounded in the natural law, so the state's power to punish is grounded in the fact that transgressions of the natural law in themselves merit proportionate punishments.

This point was made emphatically by Pope Pius XII: "When it is a question of the execution of a man condemned to death, the State does not dispose of the individual's right to live. It is then reserved to the public power to deprive the condemned of the benefit of life, in expiation of his fault, *when already, by his fault, he has dispossessed himself of the right to life*" (my emphasis). There is a direct and necessary connection between a person's transgressing the natural law and his meriting punishment for that transgression—this apart from any human convention or authority. A person who commits a murder "merits death," he becomes "worthy of death"—which is to say (it is important to note) *not* that he *must* be put to death but rather that he is in a condition such that he would be treated appropriately were he to be put to death. If only two persons existed on earth, and one of them killed the other, it would be the case that the remaining person merited death for what he did. If the death penalty were abolished in all of the countries of the earth from now until the end of time, still we could truly say, of every murderer, that he is worthy of death for his crime.

"Thou Shalt Not Kill"

There are Catholics who might admit that, in some abstract sense, a murderer deserves to die for his crime, but who would insist that the execution of that judgment belongs to God alone. To support their view, they might cite the fifth commandment, "Thou shalt not kill." Aquinas, when he considers this argument in the *Summa contra Gentiles*, calls it "frivolous," pointing out that "in the law which says 'Thou shalt not kill' there is the later statement 'Wrongdoers thou shalt not suffer to live' (Exodus 22:18). From this we are given to understand," Aquinas notes, "that the unjust execution of men is prohibited" (III, 146). The Law in fact prescribes capital punishment for murder, kidnapping, false witness in a capital charge, cursing one's parents, sexual immorality, witchcraft or magic, idolatry, blasphemy, and sacrilege. . . .

Three Factors

Three factors . . . must hold for the punishment to be licit: the punished person must be worthy of punishment; the one who punishes must have authority to do so; and the punishment must be administered for the sake of the common good. Both the theory that all punishment is therapy, and the utilitarian idea that only good consequences justify punishment, neglect the first factor and hence can serve as rationalizations for gross injustice. The theory that punishment must always be applied to the person worthy of it neglects the third factor.

Capital punishment is lawful if all three factors hold. In the case of anyone who has committed a serious crime, the first factor holds, since, as we have seen, such a person has made himself worthy of death. The second factor also holds, since the sovereign power, as we have seen, has the authority to administer punishments that are due to transgressions of the natural law. Thus the only factor that remains to be determined is: "Can the execution of this criminal reasonably be understood as contributing to the common good?" This is a question that citizens and politicians have full freedom to debate and consider, but it should never be suggested or implied that Catholics who argue in good faith that executions can contribute to the common good are departing from Church teaching or that they lack a Christian vision of society.

The Common Good

The common good is a complex thing, and we should resist all reductionist interpretations of it. For example, Aquinas lists as goods that could be aimed at in administering punishment: "that the sinner may amend, or at least that he may be restrained and others be not disturbed, that justice may be upheld, and God honored" (II-II, 108, 1, c). Only the second sort of reason typically turns up in modern discussions: it is urged, against the death penalty, that life imprisonment equally protects society. Of course life imprisonment protects neither the other prisoners nor prison guards, who are sometimes killed by imprisoned murderers. (The notorious New York State convict Willie Bosket tries to kill a guard every chance he gets.) Besides, few murderers are imprisoned for life, since society's resolve to punish a crime weakens over time: Holland even released from jail Nazi war criminals who had been given life sentences.

The other reasons Aquinas mentions seem to signify much of what defenders of capital punishment are concerned about. That a murderer repent is a good all of us can agree upon. Ted Bundy's last act was to call his mother and tell her that he was sorry for his evil deeds and felt reconciled to God. His mother's final words to him were: "You will always be my precious son." Is it not the case that, precisely because Bundy was brought face-to-face with the evil he dealt out to others and recognized publicly that he had done wrong—is it not the case that we can now, as a result of this, share in his mother's regard for him? Something occurred there, something was taught, from which we can all benefit.

Justice is of course a common good, distinct from any of the particular benefits or burdens that constitute a just state of affairs. We recognize this—with our "social justice" committees—in the case of distributive justice, but besides distributive justice there is commutative justice, which includes retributive justice. The mere fact that retributive justice is upheld is a common good and can provide a reason for punishment.

There would seem to be crimes for which only capital punishment adequately upholds justice. Such would include the "crimes against humanity" perpetrated by the Nazis and also homicide which is "outrageously or wantonly vile, horrible or inhuman," as a Georgia statute reads. These acts are offenses not only against a particular human being but also against humanity and human dignity itself. Those who commit them should be separated completely from human community, and their continued habilitation in a prison, it might be argued, would constitute toleration of and hence indirect complicity with their crimes. . . .

The Gift of Life

Finally, the death penalty testifies that life is a gift. We can see that this is so if we compare Aquinas' discussion of whether it is lawful to imprison a human being (II-II, 65, 3). The argument that it is not is that "man, having a free will, is undue matter for imprisonment which is inconsistent with free will." Clearly a similar argument could be constructed about life: a man, because he is a rational, living being, is "undue matter" for the death penalty. Aquinas replies that "A man who abuses the power entrusted to him deserves to lose it, and therefore when a man by sinning abuses the free use of his members, he becomes fitting matter for imprisonment." The corresponding reply regarding life is: a power which is entrusted to someone, as a gift, deserves to be lost if it is abused; in recognizing that the death penalty is sometimes appropriate, a society recognizes that life is a gift to be used well.

It is commonly argued that the death penalty should be abolished because it is applied more frequently to minorities and hence is discriminatory. But this is at best an argument for reforming the application of the death penalty; it does not touch the questions of whether there should be a death penalty at all. Moreover, the statistical arguments that the death penalty is not a deterrent are unpersuasive. All of the studies conclude only negatively, that there is no evidence that the death penalty is a deterrent. But surely the burden of proof lies the other way round: common sense dictates that it will be some sort of deterrent, and we are justified in acting on this conviction, until there is conclusive evidence to the contrary.

Furthermore, it is prudent to err on the side of using capital punishment. Consider the two mistakes that we could make: either we could use the death penalty as a deterrent, when in fact it is not a deterrent, or we could stop using the death penalty, when in fact it is a deterrent. The consequence of the first mistake is that guilty persons die—the criminals who are put to death. The consequence of the second mistake is that more innocent persons are murdered. Clearly we ought to err in the first way, not the second.

Similarly, in response to the argument that a few innocent persons will inevitably be put to death if capital punishment is used, it could be pointed out that, since murderers often murder again, innocent persons will also be killed if capital punishment is *not* used. However, since in the latter case the killings are intended and premeditated, they are greater evils, and so, again, it is better to make the former sort of mistake. . . .

An Ethical Ideal

There are some who argue that society might, in an extraordinary and supererogatory way, display its respect for human dignity by refraining from capital punishment. This is the approach, I believe, that is taken by the Pope. On this view, to administer the death penalty is good; to withold it, knowing that one could administer it, is better.

Protecting Innocent Life

God himself instituted the death penalty (*Genesis 9:6*) and Christ regarded capital punishment as a just penalty for murder (*Matthew 26:52*). God gave to government the legitimate authority to use capital punishment to restrain murder and punish murderers. Not to inflict the death penalty is a flagrant disregard for God's divine law which recognizes the dignity of human life as a product of God's creation. Life is sacred, and that is why God instituted the death penalty—as a way to protect innocent human life.

Reuben Hahn, *Human Events*, March 2, 1985.

Note, however, that a society may adopt this high ethical ideal only after it has understood and accepted the traditional teaching of the Church. This is a proposal to show mercy, which is possible only if the fittingness of punishment is first acknowledged. Only after someone realizes that he can lawfully inflict the death penalty can his choice to withhold it be a free act of generosity. But our society is in a very different condition; few persons understand the Church's teaching, and few of those who press for the abolition of the death penalty accept it. For us, at the present time, the abolition of the death penalty would be regress, not progress.

> *"The death penalty . . . is immoral, evil, unethical, and un-Christian."*

Christians Cannot Morally Support the Death Penalty

John Dear

Because Christian teachings call for love and forgiveness, Christians cannot support the death penalty, John Dear maintains in the following viewpoint. He believes that Christians, like Jesus, must forgive, not execute, murderers. Dear coordinates a church shelter for the homeless in Washington, D.C., and is the author of *Disarming the Heart: Toward a Vow of Nonviolence.*

As you read, consider the following questions:

1. What effect did Jesus's words have on the scribes and the Pharisees who were about to stone a woman accused of adultery, according to the author?
2. In Dear's view, how do the powerful in society use the death penalty?
3. Sometimes crowds cheer outside a prison when an execution is taking place. How does the author interpret the actions of such crowds?

John Dear, "Seventy Times Seven," *Sojourners*, August/September 1989. Reprinted with permission from *Sojourners*, PO Box 29272, Washington, DC 20017.

The gospel explains it all. Capital punishment was the rule of the land. Everyone was in on it. Death held final sway over the poor and the rebellious. If Jesus was to speak for love of life, at some point he had to speak against their love of death.

The religious men of his time brought to Jesus a woman whom they were going to stone to death, legally, for committing the crime of adultery. Her male companion, who also would have committed the adultery, was not to be killed; he was not even brought forward. When Jesus was pressed for his opinion, as they were about to stone her, he began to trace on the ground.

What he traced there has boggled the thoughtful for centuries. But it is not so much what he traced that matters but the fact that he stopped to trace on the ground at all. His calm, childlike response must have taken the scribes and Pharisees totally by surprise. It changed the center of their attention from their fury and anger to his scribbling on the ground. Once he had their attention, once they were listening and trying to figure out what he was doing, then he proceeded to give an answer, knowing they could hear it and a life might be saved.

"Let the one without sin cast the first stone."

Jesus not only condemned the death penalty, he poetically chastised the scribes and Pharisees for considering themselves sinless and able to pass judgment on others. Jesus' words made them realize their own sinfulness and filled them with shame.

His words should have the same impact on us today.

Georgia and Dachau

A few miles south of Atlanta, Georgia, just off the main interstate highway, past the McDonald's, across the street from a 200-year-old cemetery, lies the Georgia Diagnostic and Classification Center, otherwise known as death row. The grounds are maintained as well as those of an elite country club. After a half mile of travel, past the blue lake on the right, tall white towers appear in the distance, connected by white walls and chain fences that enclose a mammoth, white, windowless building. Up close, the scene is unusual and disturbing in the extreme. It immediately reminded me of Dachau.

In 1981 when I visited Dachau, the infamous Nazi concentration camp, I could not help noticing that it was situated in a typical, suburban German town. Behind all the green trees loomed a large compound cornered by tall, imposing towers, which in their heyday had been guarded by soldiers 24 hours a day. At Dachau business as usual meant death as usual. Suburban German life proceeded normally.

It is the same in Georgia and across the United States at every death row. Killing takes place inside these massive structures as a matter of routine; outside, the routine of daily life proceeds as usual. Currently, 107 people live on Georgia's death row, waiting to be killed—legally—by their government. More than 2,100 people sit on death rows in 37 states around the country. More than 5,000 people have been executed in the United States in this century; 109 have been put to death since 1977.

At the Prison

From atop a five-story white tower a voice yelled down, "What are you doing here?"

"I've come to visit a friend," I shouted back, straining to be heard.

After 30 minutes of negotiations, interviews at various security checkpoints, and a maze of long hallways and cell doors, I came upon the visitation room. I had come to Jackson, Georgia, to visit my friend, Billy Neal Moore, who has been on death row for 15 years, longer than anyone else in the United States.

Billy grew up in a poor Georgia family, married early, fathered a son, enlisted in the Army, and saw his marriage break up. He had always struggled financially. One day, after he and a friend named George Curtis had been drinking, they planned to rob the home of George's uncle. After running from the scene with George, Billy returned alone to the home of the elderly uncle. The uncle approached Billy, apparently shot at him and missed, and then hit Billy's leg with the handle of a shotgun. In a panic, Billy shot and killed him with the gun. On July 17, 1974, after waiving trial by jury, Billy was sentenced to death.

Billy was granted a stay of execution in 1978. A few years later he was baptized in a prison bathtub, resulting in Billy's feeling "for the first time in my life an experience of total acceptance and love. God's love cut through and washed the scales from my heart," he reflected afterward.

In 1984, Billy was granted a second stay, just seven hours before his scheduled execution. Petitions on Billy's behalf included pleas for clemency from six relatives of the man Billy murdered. During his first six years in prison, Billy was never allowed outside; now, he is allowed outside briefly twice a week. Over the years Billy has corresponded with more than 100 people from across the country and the world. He acts as a counselor and convener of prayer groups on death row. The courts will make a final decision regarding his life.

A Life of Faith

Billy and I have become good friends during the five years that I have known him. From the time I received his first letter, after I had written to offer a word of friendship and consolation, I have been struck by his faith. He wrote: "Your letter was appreciated and I do thank you, but know that the Lord Jesus Christ is in full control of my life."

Over the years, Billy's insights, reflections, and prayers have touched me like the letters of Paul, who Christians tend to forget was a notorious murderer before he converted to Christ and became an apostle for the faith. Billy has become a person of the Spirit and the Word, of nonviolence and love, an apostle of Christ for many of us.

And may God have mercy on our souls.

Paul Conrad, © 1990, *Los Angeles Times*. Reprinted with permission.

Ironically, Billy Neal Moore, a death row inmate, has become a teacher and model of Christian nonviolence for me. He prays with the strength of knowing that someone is listening. Rarely have I encountered such faith. "Here, on death row," he wrote to me one day, "I try to live a Christian life in ways that will get others to desire the life of Christ.

"My whole life has become a vow of nonviolence, as much as I can live," he continued. "The greatest wars and battles are in each of us, and it's only by the Holy Spirit that we can maintain peace. . . . I want to be nonviolent, so I respond kindly and respectfully to the guards and other prisoners," he told me on a visit. "I know God forgives me," he said.

"If churches really knew that the death penalty was adverse to Jesus Christ, then they wouldn't support it," Moore wrote. "So many Christians accept the salvation and forgiveness of God for themselves, yet for the people on death row there is no forgiveness at all, only death.

"People have to be reminded about the times when they did something wrong and realized it and changed," Moore wrote. "Christ is the changing agent in us all. If it can happen with them, why can't it happen with inmates on death row? The loving spirit of Christ, that changing agent, is at work in us all." No one should be killed, he concluded. We should all be given the chance to change, the chance to live.

An Addiction to Violence

Capital punishment is a sign of a deep sickness in our culture. Our culture is addicted to violence and is desperately ill. The plagues of abortion, war, racism, sexism, consumerism, apartheid, torture, and nuclear weapons are all signs of that illness in the world. The death penalty, like these other signs of society gone awry, is immoral, evil, unethical, and un-Christian.

Contrary to what its supporters claim, capital punishment—as many studies have shown—does not deter people from committing violent crime. Rather, it is used by the powerful to maintain the illusion that violent crime is under control and being disposed of. In reality, capital punishment "disposes of" the poor, primarily the black poor. Rich people who commit murder can hire lawyers to get them off death row. The poor are the ones who are killed on death row, and the government spends millions of dollars killing them. As Moore explained: "Since I've been on death row, the government has spent more than $1 million preparing for my death. If I had just a fraction of that money originally, I wouldn't be here. That's what I was looking for when I was young."

The death penalty is racist. According to the National Coalition to Abolish the Death Penalty, in a six-year period in Georgia, 39 percent of capital murder cases involved white victims, yet 84 percent of the death sentences imposed were in those cases with white victims. During that same period, black defendants were charged with 23 percent of murders of white victims, yet blacks received 46 percent of the death sentences imposed in those cases. Black defendants charged with killing white victims were 11 times more likely to be sentenced to death. Such discrimination exists not only in Georgia but everywhere the death penalty is used. Ninety percent of those on death row are there for killing white people, although each year almost half of homicide victims are black.

The death penalty is a slow form of torture, culminating in murder—the premeditated, meticulously legal killing of a human being by another human being—and by the entire society.

Capital punishment, like all violence, is inconsistent and illogical. In this case, society justifies capital punishment to set an "example" for those who kill. Approximately 20,000 people are murdered each year in this country, and 4,000 are convicted of murdering others. Out of that group, slightly more than 2,100 are sentenced to death.

All Are Children of God

As Christians, we must recognize in every human being the presence of God. The scripture is explicit about this: God is in each one of us. We are all children of God, all redeemable. Particularly, Christ comes to us in the distressing guise of the poor, in our enemies, in the unborn, in prisoners. Followers of Jesus are therefore a pro-life people who side with any victim of violence, always resist death, and promote human life for all through steadfast mercy and compassion.

The challenge for us today is to take seriously Jesus' words on death and sin and forgiveness. The challenge is to hear the voice of God in the death row inmate saying, "Killing is wrong. Christians should not kill."

Our word is a word of forgiveness and life. We are asked to forgive and offer hospitality to the murderer, as Ananias was asked to accept Saul—the notorious murderer—into his house, where Saul became the beloved apostle Paul (Acts 9:10-19). Unfortunately, as Martin Luther King Jr. observed, "Capital punishment is society's final statement that we will not forgive."

Jesus' retort to capital punishment speaks to our common sinfulness. "Let the one without sin . . . " challenges those of us who think we are not sinful. In reality, all people are sinners. This is part of our original sin. Even if we have not actually killed someone physically, like Billy Neal Moore has, we are guilty of participating in and supporting a system that has murdered thousands, indeed millions, of people in more than 100 wars during this century.

From God's perspective, we are all guilty. Not one of us is without sin. Like the crowd wanting to stone the adulterous woman, we should simply walk away from the idea of killing someone on death row, ashamed of ourselves. Jesus breaks the limits set by society on how much we are allowed to forgive others—by forgiving everyone.

Capital punishment is as legal today as it was 2,000 years ago when Jesus was legally executed. Today we have the choice to stand with the executed, as Jesus did and Paul learned to, or the executioners, as Pilate and Herod did.

A Nonviolent Ethic

For followers of Jesus, the only consistent ethic of life is the nonviolent ethic of the cross, the way of life that chooses to side with victims of injustice. Jesus taught his followers that true discipleship to him means not only not inflicting the penalty of death on others but risking the death penalty for oneself. The symbol of discipleship in the early community became the cross, which translates today into the electric chair.

In the Image of God

The Judeo-Christian heritage has been consistent over the centuries in teaching that murder is an immoral act. A consensus has emerged among every major religious body which has a position on the issue that the death penalty contravenes this tradition and should be abandoned. Thus the religious community has coincided with the official position of every Western democracy—except the United States—in moving towards an abolition of the death penalty.

One of the reasons for the Judeo-Christian anti-death penalty tradition has been the realization that each person is a child of God. If each soul is endowed with the image of God, then society would do well to respect such a reality and not destroy it through the process of state-sanctioned killing.

Joseph B. Ingle, *The Witness*, November 1989.

The nonviolent ethic of the cross is a way of loving our enemies and all those whom the state condemns to death: the poor, the unborn, those on death row. We are to offer the healing hand of redemption to everyone, including those who the state says can no longer be redeemed.

We have to question—peacefully, respectfully, nonviolently—the people who have the power to kill others. Jesus questioned those who held the stones in their hands. We are asked to do the same, to confront the people who enforce this policy of death with the words, "Let the one without sin be the first to throw the switch."

The photos of cheering crowds at the places of executions are signs that our society lacks the desire to rise above such barbarism and violence. As long as people cheer and mock the murder of any human being, as long as they pay for it with their tax dollars, as long as they continue to do business as usual while the government executes people in prisons across the country, the killing and brutality will never end.

We are called to see Billy Neal Moore and everyone else on death row as Christ present in the world. We are invited to a radical forgiveness and healing, to forgive as God forgives others, to allow others to live. We are called to forgive 70 times seven times, not just those everyday small annoyances that others do to us, but cold-blooded murder as well—even the murder of our loved ones. We are called to forgive the murderer as Christ forgives the murderer, as Christ forgives us. We are called to be reconciled with those who have injured us (Matthew 5:43-45) and to pray for forgiveness for our sins "as we forgive those who have sinned against us" (Matthew 6:12).

We must offer sympathy and support for the victims of violent crime and their families; we must also offer the compassion of Christ to those on death row and prevent their murder.

A Change of Heart

My visit with Billy Neal Moore ended with a prayer that God would enter into the hearts of us all and help us to choose life. Billy Neal Moore and others on death row continue that Gethsemane prayer vigil and invite us to undergo the change of heart that Billy has already undergone.

"It is simply unrealistic and silly to insist that no one under eighteen can be held fully accountable."

Executing Juvenile Murderers Is Just

Ernest van den Haag

Ernest van den Haag is a former John M. Olin professor of jurisprudence and public policy at Fordham University in Bronx, New York. In the following viewpoint, van den Haag argues that the death penalty is a just punishment for many juvenile murderers. While some juveniles may not be mature enough to understand the severity of their crimes, van den Haag believes that society has a right and a duty to execute those who are.

As you read, consider the following questions:

1. What does the author believe will be the consequences of protecting juvenile murderers from execution?
2. Why does van den Haag favor allowing juries to determine which juvenile should be executed?
3. Why does the author oppose attempts at rehabilitating juvenile murderers?

Ernest van den Haag, "Young Murderers." This article appeared in the November 1989 issue and is reprinted with permission from *The World & I*, a publication of The Washington Times Corporation, copyright © 1989.

A majority of Americans—more than 70 percent according to polls—favor the death penalty for murderers. However, many judges, lawyers (execution reduces the pool of clients) and, above all, law professors oppose it. Unable to persuade the voters, they tried for many years to get the Supreme Court to declare the death penalty unconstitutional. The court refused, but it did prohibit the execution of persons who were under sixteen when they murdered.

Abolitionists now want to raise the minimum age to eighteen —a two-year difference. (Some want to raise the age still further.) Abolitionists obviously want to apply the death penalty to as few murderers as possible. Yet most murders are committed by very young people. Immunizing them against the death penalty means that they will be able to murder again in prison and out; further, the group most inclined to murder—male youths—would not be threatened with the most severe penalty. People mature earlier now than they did in the past; yet we hold them accountable for their actions later, if at all. This hardly makes sense.

Distinguishing Right from Wrong

Obviously a small child may not understand the effect of his acts and, therefore, not intend them. A child also may not be able to tell right from wrong or understand that any act is morally and legally wrong. For either reason, children below the age of reason are not held criminally responsible, although they are usually subject to minor punishment by parents and teachers. As children grow, they learn. A sixteen-year-old, unless severely retarded, knows that shooting can kill the victim and that murder is regarded as morally and legally wrong. He understands what he is doing when he murders and that it is wrong; that understanding does not begin on his eighteenth birthday. (I think understanding on the average begins before sixteen, but the Supreme Court has drawn a line that other courts cannot disregard.) To be sure, some juvenile murderers, although aware of the wrongness of their act, may not have a very deep understanding of it; or they may be impulsive or emotionally immature. So may older murderers. That is why juries weigh all relevant factors before deciding whether capital punishment is appropriate or not.

Each case is different. While some juvenile murderers are quite immature, others are quite mature. Our criminal justice system accommodates these differences. In capital trials, upon conviction, the jury weighs the mitigating and aggravating factors in a separate proceeding. It can impose the death penalty only if it finds that the murder was particularly heinous and that the aggravating factors outweigh the mitigating ones. Surely, if the jury

83

feels that the juvenile murderer did not understand the meaning of the act, the jury will not impose the death penalty. But it is simply unrealistic and silly to insist that no one under eighteen can be held fully accountable. Some seventeen-year-olds are quite mature, just as some twenty-five-year-olds are not.

© Markstein/Copley News Service. Reprinted with permission.

After listening to prosecution and defense, and to psychiatric experts if desired, juries can be trusted to come to a fair judgment. Juries are quite sparing with the death penalty. Out of twenty thousand annual homicides, fewer than three hundred lead to death sentences. The execution of juvenile murderers has always been exceptional. Three were executed in the last ten years—about two hundred thousand homicides were committed over that period by people of all ages. Ruling—as abolitionists propose—that no one under eighteen can be held fully responsible is just as bad as ruling that everyone can be. Surely a jury is best able to give due weight to the relevant individual features that may or may not call for the death penalty. It should retain the power to do so.

Let me consider briefly some objections to the death penalty for those between sixteen and eighteen. Whether the death penalty deters more than life imprisonment without parole is controversial. Although some abolitionists assert the contrary, no one has argued, let alone proved, that execution deters less than imprisonment. Death is the end; but where there is life, even in prison, there always is hope. Common sense tells us that fear of death is likely to be greater than fear of life in prison. Further, we do not have life imprisonment without parole in most states. Temporary imprisonment certainly is a lesser deterrent than the death penalty.

Execution does prevent rehabilitation. The data clearly indicate that rehabilitation, although possible, is not probable on the average for most criminals of any age. There is no serious evidence showing that juveniles are rehabilitated more readily than other persons. In any event, we never know—until it is too late —whether a murderer actually has been rehabilitated. His victim cannot be rehabilitated. Why should the murderer have a chance to be? Murder does not call for a second chance.

Other Objections

There are other objections to the death penalty for juveniles: trials are costly; racial discrimination may come into play; execution is physically the same act as homicide. However, these are the same arguments used against the death penalty for people over twenty-one. They have been refuted so often and so completely by both data and argument that refuting them once more would be redundant.

"The death penalty is cruel and unusual punishment when applied to persons under eighteen years of age."

Executing Juvenile Murderers Is Unjust

Glenn M. Bieler

In the following viewpoint, Glenn M. Bieler contends that the death penalty is too severe a punishment for juvenile murderers. Bieler believes that juveniles are too immature to understand the consequences of their actions, and because of this they should be held less accountable for their crimes. In addition, he argues that the death penalty has no deterrent effect on juveniles because they usually do not plan their crimes. The author is a graduate of New York Law School and an attorney in New York City.

As you read, consider the following questions:

1. What examples does the author give to support his belief that legislatures recognize the inability of minors to make responsible decisions?
2. What factors often cause adolescents to perform potentially destructive acts, according to Bieler?
3. Why does the author believe that retribution is not a good reason for society to execute juveniles?

This viewpoint is an edited version of "Death Be Not Proud: A Note on Juvenile Capital Punishment," by Glenn M. Bieler, *New York Law School Journal of Human Rights*, vol. 7, no. 2, 1990. Reprinted with permission.

"Texan Put to Death for a Murder Committed at 17"
"South Carolina Executes Killer, Age Stirs Protest—Pleas for Man Convicted at 17 are rejected"
"Texas Man Executed By Lethal Injection in Deaths of Women"

Mention the death penalty and arguments abound. Proponents claim the threat of death deters severe criminal behavior. Opponents claim that society should not advocate an "eye-for-an-eye" approach to sentencing. This paper discusses not the death penalty itself but its application to a specific class of persons: juveniles who kill.

Juvenile capital punishment has become one of the major controversial issues to unfold in the last decade. This issue adds a new dimension to the emotional debates surrounding the death penalty. While it seems likely that death sentences will continue to be rendered, the question becomes to what extreme will society go to allow the imposition of such a penalty. In other words, does the death penalty become cruel and unusual punishment in violation of the eighth amendment to the United States Constitution when a juvenile offender is involved? . . .

Modern principles of law dictate that no persons should be sentenced to death unless they are at least eighteen years of age. The Supreme Court's creation of a gap between ages sixteen and eighteen falls short of contemporary standards of decency which mark a progressing society. By creating such a gap, the Court has failed to acknowledge that all "children have a special place in life which the law should reflect.". . .

The Juvenile's Reduced Culpability

It has long been recognized that juveniles and adults do not share equal responsibility for their crimes. That juveniles possess a reduced culpability in committing crimes is a basic standard accepted by our legal system. . . . The general societal belief that juvenile and adult criminals be treated differently should apply with equal force to the death penalty. Three areas which support this proposition are the state's duty as *parens patriae* to protect minors, the arbitrary nature of the waiver system from juvenile court into adult court, and "time of life" aspects of adolescence which makes juveniles more susceptible than adults to committing crimes (including murder), yet less culpable than adults in terms of punishment.

The power of the state to act as *parens patriae* in protecting its minors has long been recognized by the Supreme Court. In *Bellotti v. Baird*, a case involving a minor's right to have an abortion without the need for parental or judicial consent, the Court noted that:

> [s]tates . . . may limit the freedom of children to choose for themselves in the making of important, affirmative choices

87

with potentially serious consequences . . . *during the formative years of childhood and adolescence, minors often lack the experience, perspective, and judgment to recognize and avoid choices that could be detrimental to them.*

State and federal legislatures also recognize the inherent difficulty of minors to make responsible decisions. For instance, people under eighteen are not allowed to vote, serve as jurors, or join the armed forces. The premise behind such deprivations (which, if applied to adults, would necessarily have constitutional implications) is that minors are not possessed with the full capacity to make individual choices. Therefore, it is difficult to understand how states can execute minors. Can a state at one moment say that minors are incapable of making adult decisions, then at the next moment say that minors should be held as responsible as adults for their acts? Such a standard of convenience should not be tolerated when it involves criminal punishment. As the Court stated in *Eddings v. Oklahoma*:

> Crimes committed by youths may be just as harmful to victims as those committed by older persons, but they [the crimes] deserve less punishment because adolescents may have less capacity to control their conduct and to think in long-range terms than adults. Moreover, youth crime as such is not exclusively the offender's fault; offenses by the young also represent a failure of family, school, and the social system, which share the responsibility for the development of America's youth. . . .

Adolescents are egotists. They often view their opinions as being right and other contradictory opinions as being wrong. This special feeling leads to a belief in immortality and allows the adolescent to dehumanize others into abstract objects rather than human beings. Adolescence is characterized by emotion rather than rationality. These youngsters often live for the moment with little thought of future consequences for their present actions. They typically have not yet learned to accept the finality of death. Together, a feeling of omnipotence and an inability to fear death contributes to the adolescent performing potentially destructive acts like attempting suicide, taking dangerous drugs, racing cars, and other hazardous behaviors.

The Victims of Violence

Adolescents who murder usually suffer additional handicaps. Studies of homicidal minors reveal that these juveniles are frequently subjected to intense emotional deprivation and physical violence in their homes. In many instances, the child suffers severe and repeated physical abuse. Frequent brutal fights between the child's parents are commonplace. In addition, substance abuse by one or both parents often figures prominently in the childhood of the juvenile murderer. Also, such adolescents tend to be intellectually immature and educationally deficient, and are more apt to exhibit signs of paranoia and illogical thoughts than nonviolent youths. Juvenile murderers may also be suffering from some sort of chronological impairment which oftentimes may be impossible to diagnose until the juvenile has aged.

A clinical study was performed on juvenile murderers who live on death row. The juveniles used in the study were chosen exclusively because of their age at the time they committed murder.

Reprinted by permission of Mike Luckovich and Creators Syndicate.

The study found many similarities between these young offenders. Background histories included difficulties at birth, head injuries, illnesses, drug overdoses known to affect the central nervous system, loss of consciousness, fainting, blackouts or other lapses, and seizures and symptoms suggestive of psychomotor epilepsy. All fourteen juveniles exhibited psychiatric disturbances of some sort. Twelve of the fourteen subjects also had I.Q. [intelligence quotient] scores below ninety. The study concluded that: the multiple battering suffered by these youths sometimes caused actual brain damage which resulted in increased impulsiveness; the severe parental violence functioned as a model for the youth's abnormal behavior; and the extreme brutality to which the youth was exposed promoted rage which was displaced onto other individuals in their environment. These conclusions are persuasive evidence that such juveniles should not be held fully responsible for their acts.

Adolescence is "the period of physical and psychological development from the onset of puberty to maturity." It is the transitional period between childhood and adulthood. This stage of life lasts roughly from age twelve to age nineteen. While it can be argued that all murderers, adult and juvenile, suffer the same emotional turmoil, the primary difference is that juveniles have not had the time to mature or been given the chance to change. There is a presumption still existing for persons within the stage of adolescence that they have not developed the judgment, fully formed identity, or character of adults. If punishment is to be "directly related to the personal culpability of the criminal defendant," this correlation does not justify the imposition of a death sentence on juveniles.

Justifications of the Death Penalty

The reduced culpability of the juvenile also negates the two penal justifications for having the death penalty—general deterrence and retribution. As the Court previously held, the death penalty has little deterrent effect against defendants who have a reduced capacity for considered choice since such persons are unlikely to precede their murderous acts with "cold calculus" of thought. And even where it can be said that juveniles do calculate, the fear of death will not be a deterrent since such young offenders have not yet learned to accept the finality of death.

Retribution, which the Court defines as "the expression of society's moral outrage at particularly offensive conduct," is also an unsatisfactory justification for the juvenile death penalty. Retribution goes to the degree of culpability of the offense and not the extent of the injury on the victim. By sentencing youths to death, society is inflicting an irreversible form of punishment on a class of persons whose degree of responsibility mandates less severe measures. . . .

Murder is appalling whether it is committed by a juvenile or an adult. No one will argue that assumption. However, it must be remembered that punishment is determined by the degree of culpability of the offender. The fact that juveniles are less responsible than adults for their crimes makes the imposition of the death penalty on this class of persons unjust. . . . The death penalty is cruel and unusual punishment when applied to persons under eighteen years of age. Society's killer instinct should not be deemed legal until the offender is held in the same regard.

Determining a Punishment for Murder

Juries are largely responsible for determining which criminals are sentenced to death in the United States. Because of this important role, much of the controversy surrounding the death penalty focuses on the ability of jurors to hand down impartial and just decisions.

In the following activity, you and your classmates will be members of a jury. Together you must decide if a defendant guilty of murder should be sentenced to death or to life imprisonment. This activity will give you a better understanding of how a real jury reaches a similar decision. It may also help you understand the difficulty in assigning just punishments.

1. Form a group of twelve or fewer students. Select one student in your group as the jury foreman or forewoman. This student must ensure that the debate remains calm, logical, and focused on the facts of the case. While a real jury may take hours, days, or weeks to reach a decision, your foreman or forewoman should guide your jury to a decision within thirty minutes.

2. The jury foreman or forewoman should read the following jury instructions aloud, or the jurors should read the instructions carefully to themselves.

Jury Instructions

A. *Aggravating Factors*

Every state has a list of aggravating factors—details about a crime that are required for a jury to determine a sentence of death. While these aggravating factors vary from state to state, the following is a typical list of such factors. You the jury may sentence the defendant to death *only* if he or she committed the murder while also committing one of the following crimes:

a) rape;
b) kidnapping;
c) burglary;
d) armed robbery.

If none of the above factors apply to the defendant's crime, you may not sentence the defendant to death.

B. *Mitigating Factors*

Every state also has a list of mitigating factors—details about the defendant or the crime that might provide just reason for not handing down a death sentence. Decide if any of the mitigating factors listed below apply to the defendant. You may decide that the mitigating factors that apply outweigh any aggravating factors. In this case, you would sentence the defendant to life imprisonment. However, you may decide that no mitigating factors apply, or that those that do apply do not outweigh the aggravating factors. In either of these last two cases, you would sentence the defendant to death. Balance the aggravating factors above with the following mitigating factors:

1) the defendant has no significant history of violent crime;
2) the murder was committed while the defendant was mentally or emotionally disturbed;
3) the defendant was an accomplice in the murder committed by another person and his or her participation was relatively minor;
4) the defendant acted under duress or under the domination of another person;
5) the defendant was incapable of understanding the criminality of his or her conduct;
6) the defendant was younger than sixteen or suffered from mental illness or mental retardation at the time of the crime;
7) the defendant was provoked by the victim into committing the murder.

In addition, you may consider any other mitigating factors you find relevant.

As jurors you must evaluate the evidence and determine which evidence is most reliable. If any aggravating factors (A) exist and outweigh the mitigating factors (B), you may sentence the defendant to death. If you find no aggravating factors, or if you judge that the mitigating factors outweigh the aggravating factors, you may sentence the defendant to life imprisonment. In arriving at a verdict, the jury must be unanimous. If the sentence is death, the foreman or forewoman must list the aggravating circumstance(s) which the jury found to apply beyond a reasonable doubt. The foreman or forewoman must also indicate if the jury is unable to reach a unanimous verdict (a situation known as a "hung jury").

3. Read the following case.

The Case

Matthew Williams, Karen Stacey, and Lee Bruoni have been convicted of the armed robbery of a convenience store and the murder of the clerk, twenty-one-year-old Charles Robertson. The defendants testify that they entered the store around 11 p.m., waited until the other customers left, and then ordered Robertson to empty the cash drawer. Robertson emptied the drawer of $115 and gave the money to Stacey. One of the defendants then shot and killed Robertson. The defendants escaped in Williams' car. A witness spotted the defendants leaving the store, called police, and later identified the defendants. Bruoni is a seventeen-year-old high school dropout. Stacey is a twenty-year-old high school graduate who enrolled in but then dropped out of college. Williams is a nineteen-year-old college freshman who provided the car used in the crime. He testifies that he became involved with Stacey and met Bruoni through her, against the advice of his parents. He insists the other two convinced him to go along with them and that Stacey and Bruoni planned the entire crime. Stacey and Bruoni both testify that the crime was actually suggested by Williams. Stacey claims Bruoni fired the fatal shot impulsively when Robertson made a sudden move; Bruoni says Williams planned and committed the murder; Williams insists Stacey pulled the trigger. All three defendants are white; the victim was black. None of the defendants has had any prior convictions for violent crime.

4. You the jury have already convicted all three defendants of armed robbery and murder. Using the jury instructions as a guideline, determine a sentence for each defendant.

5. Compare your jury's decision with the decisions of the other juries in the class. Discuss the factors each jury took into consideration. If a jury was unable to reach a unanimous decision, discuss why.

6. Discuss the beliefs you held about the death penalty prior to this activity. Did these beliefs and the beliefs of other jurors affect your jury's decision? How? Should jurors' individual opinions about the validity of the death penalty be allowed to influence their objective evaluation of evidence and, hence, their verdict?

7. From this experience, do you think juries can hand down just sentences? Explain your answer.

Periodical Bibliography

The following articles have been selected to supplement the diverse views presented in this chapter.

George N. Boyd — "Capital Punishment: Deserved and Wrong," *The Christian Century*, February 17, 1988.

Edmund G. Brown with Dick Adler — "Private Mercy," *Common Cause Magazine*, July/August 1989.

Christian Social Action — "In the Valley of the Shadow: A Special Issue on the Death Penalty," November 1990. Available from the General Board of Church and Society of the United Methodist Church, 100 Maryland Ave. NE, Washington, DC 20002.

Jim Christie — "At Last, Punishment Fits the Crime," *Los Angeles Times*, March 29, 1990.

John G. Healey — "Abolish the Death Penalty," *The World & I*, November 1989.

Richard Lacayo — "The Politics of Life and Death," *Time*, April 2, 1990.

Robert W. Lee — "Cruel and Unusual Leniency," *The New American*, August 13, 1990. Available from The Review of the News Incorporated, 770 Westhill Blvd., Appleton, WI 54915.

John F. McManus — "Surgical Effect of Death Penalty," *The New American*, August 13, 1990.

The New Republic — "Burning Question," February 20, 1989.

Omni — "Stiff Sentence," February 1988.

Charley Reese — "Executed Killers Kill No More," *Conservative Chronicle*, February 15, 1989. Available from PO Box 11297, Des Moines, IA 50340-1297.

Lynn Scarlett — "Capital Punishment: No," *Reason*, June 1990. Available from Reason Foundation, 2716 Ocean Park Blvd., Suite 1062, Santa Monica, CA 90405.

Walter Shapiro — "A Life in His Hands," *Time*, May 28, 1990.

Victor L. Streib — "An Unjust Punishment? The Juvenile Death Penalty," *The World & I*, April 1990.

Dick Thompson — "Bad News for Death Row," *Time*, July 10, 1989.

Is the Death Penalty an Effective Punishment?

Chapter Preface

While the death penalty debate often revolves around arguments of morality and justice, another large part of the controversy focuses on the death penalty's effectiveness as a punishment. An effective punishment, according to many experts, not only penalizes the criminal but deters crime, protects the public, and helps provide restitution to the victims of the crime and to society as a whole. Whether the death penalty meets any of these requirements is a subject of debate.

Proponents of the death penalty believe it is effective for several reasons. Execution protects the public by preventing a criminal from ever murdering again, they contend, whereas imprisoned murderers may escape, kill other inmates, kill prison guards, or be released into society again. Death penalty supporters also firmly believe that executions deter others from committing murder. "There can be no stronger deterrent than the threat of death," states Ernest van den Haag, a former John M. Olin professor of jurisprudence and public policy at Fordham University. In addition, while nothing can restore the life of a murder victim, death penalty proponents believe that the murderer's death is effective in proving to the victim's family and society as a whole that the taking of life is so heinous that it must be paid for by death.

Many Americans, however, view the death penalty as an ineffective punishment. Death penalty opponents assert that there is no evidence that proves the death penalty deters crime. In fact, countries without the death penalty generally have lower crime rates than those with it, they maintain. Thorsten Sellin, a noted researcher on the deterrent effect of the death penalty, found that "executions have no discernible effect on homicide death rates." Death penalty opponents believe that because executions do not deter murder, they are the unnecessary taking of life by the state. In addition, opponents contend that executions do nothing to ease the grief of victims' families. Norman Felton, whose daughter, granddaughter, and son-in-law were murdered by drug addicts, argues that executing the murderer does not even restore a family's belief in justice. Felton says he believes in "positive things to heal. . . . Executing [murderers] is no place to start."

Public protection, deterrence, and restitution are all factors to be considered when evaluating a punishment. The following chapter debates the effectiveness of the death penalty in meeting these criteria.

"Life sentences do not adequately protect society, whereas the death penalty properly applied does so with certainty."

The Death Penalty Is an Effective Punishment

Robert W. Lee

Robert W. Lee is a contributing editor to the conservative magazine *The New American* and the author of *The UN Conspiracy*. In the following viewpoint, Lee states that the death penalty is the only effective way to punish murderers and deter violent crime. He maintains that death sentences are handed down fairly and impartially, and that it is society's right and duty to protect the innocent and punish the guilty by means of the death penalty.

As you read, consider the following questions:

1. Why does the author believe it is impossible to accurately evaluate the death penalty's deterrent effect?
2. What factors does Lee blame for the expensive cost of death penalty prosecutions?
3. What comparison does the author make between self-defense and capital punishment?

Robert W. Lee, "Deserving to Die," *The New American*, August 13, 1990. Reprinted with permission.

A key issue in the debate over capital punishment is whether or not it is an effective deterrent to violent crime. In at least one important respect, it unquestionably is: It simply cannot be contested that a killer, once executed, is forever deterred from killing again. The deterrent effect on others, however, depends largely on how swiftly and surely the penalty is applied. Since capital punishment has not been used with any consistency over the years, it is virtually impossible to evaluate its deterrent effect accurately. Abolitionists claim that a lack of significant difference between the murder rates for states with and without capital punishment proves that the death penalty does not deter. But the states with the death penalty on their books have used it so little over the years as to preclude any meaningful comparison between states. Through July 18, 1990 there had been 134 executions since 1976. Only 14 states (less than 40 percent of those that authorize the death penalty) were involved. Any punishment, including death, will cease to be an effective deterrent if it is recognized as mostly bluff. Due to costly delays and endless appeals, the death penalty has been largely turned into a paper tiger by the same crowd that calls for its abolition on the grounds that it is not an effective deterrent!

People Fear Death

To allege that capital punishment, if imposed consistently and without undue delay, would not be a deterrent to crime is, in essence, to say that people are not afraid of dying. If so, as columnist Jenkin Lloyd Jones once observed, then warning signs reading "Slow Down," "Bridge Out," and "Danger—40,000 Volts" are futile relics of an age gone by when men feared death. To be sure, the death penalty could never become a 100-percent deterrent to heinous crime, because the fear of death varies among individuals. Some race automobiles, climb mountains, parachute jump, walk circus highwires, ride Brahma bulls in rodeos, and otherwise engage in endeavors that are more than normally hazardous. But, as author Bernard Cohen notes in his book *Law and Order*, "there are even more people who refrain from participating in these activities mainly because risking their lives is not to their taste."

Merit System

On occasion, circumstances *have* led to meaningful statistical evaluations of the death penalty's deterrent effect. In Utah, for instance, there have been three executions since the Supreme Court's 1976 ruling:

• Gary Gilmore faced a firing squad at the Utah State Prison on January 17, 1977. There had been 55 murders in the Beehive State during 1976 (4.5 per 100,000 population). During 1977, in the wake of the Gilmore execution, there were 44 murders (3.5 per 100,000), a 20 percent decrease.

• More than a decade later, on August 28, 1987, Pierre Dale Selby (one of the two infamous "hi-fi killers" who in 1974 forced five persons in an Ogden hi-fi shop to drink liquid drain cleaner, kicked a ballpoint pen into the ear of one, then killed three) was executed. During all of 1987, there were 54 murders (3.2 per 100,000). The count for January through August was 38 (a monthly average of 4.75). For September-December (in the aftermath of the Selby execution) there were 16 (4.0 per month, a nearly 16 percent decrease). For July and August there were six and seven murders, respectively. In September (the first month following Selby's demise) there were three.

Chuck Asay, by permission of the *Colorado Springs Gazette-Telegraph*.

• Arthur Gary Bishop, who sodomized and killed a number of young boys, was executed on June 10, 1988. For all of 1988 there were 47 murders (2.7 per 100,000, the fewest since 1977). During January-June, there were 26; for July-December (after the Bishop execution) the tally was 21 (a 19 percent difference). In the wake of all three Utah executions, there have been notable decreases in both the number and the rate of murders within the state. To be sure, there are other variables that could have influenced the results, but the figures are there and abolitionists to date have tended simply to ignore them.

Deterrence should never be considered the *primary* reason for administering the death penalty. It would be both immoral and unjust to punish one man merely as an example to others. The basic consideration should be: Is the punishment deserved? If not, it should not be administered regardless of what its deterrent impact might be. After all, once deterrence supersedes justice as the basis for a criminal sanction, the guilt or innocence of the accused becomes largely irrelevant. Deterrence can be achieved as effectively by executing an innocent person as a guilty one (something that communists and other totalitarians discovered long ago). If a punishment administered to one person deters someone else from committing a crime, fine. But that result should be viewed as a bonus of justice properly applied, not as a reason for the punishment. The decisive consideration should be: Has the accused *earned* the penalty?

The Cost of Execution

The exorbitant financial expense of death penalty cases is regularly cited by abolitionists as a reason for abolishing capital punishment altogether. They prefer to ignore, however, the extent to which they themselves are responsible for the interminable legal maneuvers that run up the costs.

A 1982 study by the abolitionist New York State Defenders Association—based on proposed (but never enacted) legislation to reinstate capital punishment in New York (Governor Mario Cuomo has vetoed death penalty legislation seven times in recent years)—speculated that a capital case involving only the first three levels of review (trial and penalty, appeal to the state Court of Appeals, and review by the U.S. Supreme Court) would cost $1.8 million per case, compared to the projected cost of imprisoning a felon for 40 years of $602,000. In another study, the *Miami Herald* calculated that it had cost Florida taxpayers $57.2 million to execute 18 men ($3.17 million each), whereas keeping a prisoner in jail for life (40 years) costs $515,996 ($12,899.91 per year). Abolitionists tend, we suspect, to exaggerate death-penalty costs while understating the expense of life imprisonment. According to the Justice Department, for instance, it costs around $20,000 a year to house a prisoner ($1 million over 40 years). Other sources peg it as high as $25,000.

As presently pursued, death-penalty prosecutions *are* outrageously expensive. But, again, the cost is primarily due to redundant appeals, time-consuming delays, bizarre court rulings, and legal histrionics by defense attorneys:

• Willie Darden, who had already survived three death warrants, was scheduled to die in Florida's electric chair on

September 4, 1985 for a murder he had committed in 1973. Darden's lawyer made a last-minute emergency appeal to the Supreme Court, which voted against postponing the execution until a formal appeal could be filed. So the attorney (in what he later described as "last-minute ingenuity") then requested that the emergency appeal be technically transformed into a formal appeal. Four Justices agreed (enough to force the full court to review the appeal) and the execution was stayed. After additional years of delay and expense, Darden was eventually put out of our misery on March 15, 1988. . . .

Preserving the Social Contract

The first principle of any society, and especially our own, is the absolute sovereignty of a person over his or her body. People adhere to a society so that they can be protected in their enjoyment of their quiet sovereignty and they give up some of their rights to do and act as they please in consideration for the social contract and to enjoy the benefit of protection.

When imposing the death penalty upon the murderer, society, in the form of the government, is doing only what it must do to preserve the peace and fulfill the contract.

Frank V. Kelly, *New York State Bar Journal*, July 1989.

• On April 2, 1974 William Neal Moore shot and killed a man in Georgia. Following his arrest, he pleaded guilty to armed robbery and murder and was convicted and sentenced to death. On July 20, 1975 the Georgia Supreme Court denied his petition for review. On July 16, 1976 the U.S. Supreme Court denied his petition for review. On May 13, 1977 the Jefferson County Superior Court turned down a petition for a new sentencing hearing (the state Supreme Court affirmed the denial, and the U.S. Supreme Court again denied a review). On March 30, 1978 a Tattnall County Superior Court judge held a hearing on a petition alleging sundry grounds for a writ of *habeas corpus*, but declined on July 13, 1978 to issue a writ. On October 17, 1978 the state Supreme Court declined to review that ruling. Moore petitioned the U.S. District Court for Southern Georgia. After a delay of more than two years, a U.S. District Court judge granted the writ on April 29, 1981. After another two-year delay, the 11th U.S. Circuit Court of Appeals upheld the writ on June 23, 1983. On September 30, 1983 the Circuit Court reversed itself and ruled that the writ should be denied. On March 5, 1984 the Supreme Court rejected the case for the third time.

Moore's execution was set for May 24, 1984. On May 11, 1984

his attorneys filed a petition in Butts County Superior Court, but a writ was denied. The same petition was filed in the U.S. District Court for Georgia's Southern District on May 18th, but both a writ and a stay of execution were denied. Then, on May 23rd (the day before the scheduled execution) the 11th Circuit Court of Appeals granted a stay. On June 4, 1984 a three-judge panel of the Circuit Court voted to deny a writ. After another delay of more than three years, the Circuit Court voted 7 to 4 to override its three-judge panel and rule in Moore's favor. On April 18, 1988, the Supreme Court accepted the case. On April 17, 1989 it sent the case back to the 11th Circuit Court for review in light of new restrictions that the High Court had placed on *habeas corpus*. On September 28, 1989 the Circuit Court ruled 6 to 5 that Moore had abused the writ process. On December 18, 1989 Moore's attorneys again appealed to the Supreme Court.

Moore's case was described in detail in *Insight* magazine for February 12, 1990. By the end of 1989, his case had gone through 20 separate court reviews, involving some 118 state and federal judges. It had been to the Supreme Court and back four times. There had been a substantial turnover of his attorneys, creating an excuse for one team of lawyers to file a petition claiming that all of the prior attorneys had given ineffective representation. No wonder capital cases cost so much! . . .

Lifetime to Escape

Is life imprisonment an adequate substitute for the death penalty? Presently, according to the polls, approximately three-fourths of the American people favor capital punishment. But abolitionists try to discount that figure by claiming that support for the death penalty weakens when life imprisonment without the possibility of parole is offered as an alternative. (At other times, abolitionists argue that parole is imperative to give "lifers" some hope for the future and deter their violent acts in prison.)

Life imprisonment is a flawed alternative to the death penalty, if for no other reason than that so many "lifers" escape. Many innocent persons have died at the hands of men previously convicted and imprisoned for murder, supposedly for "life." The ways in which flaws in our justice system, combined with criminal ingenuity, have worked to allow "lifers" to escape include these recent examples: . . .

• Brothers Linwood and James Briley were executed in Virginia on October 12, 1984 and April 18, 1985, respectively. Linwood had murdered a disc jockey in 1979 during a crime spree. During the same spree, James raped and killed a woman (who was eight months pregnant) and killed her five-year-old son. On May 31, 1984, the Briley brothers organized and led an escape of five death-row inmates (the largest death-row breakout in

U.S. history). They were at large for 19 days.
• On February 11, 1990 six convicts, including three murderers, escaped from their segregation cells in the maximum security Joliet Correctional Center in Illinois by cutting through bars on their cells, breaking a window, and crossing a fence. In what may be the understatement of the year, a prison spokesman told reporters: "Obviously, this is a breach of security."

Benefits of the Death Penalty

There are three good things about capital punishment. One, the killer gets to experience the same fear and agony he inflicted on others. Two, the recidivism rate for executed murderers is zero. Three, electricity (or rope or bullets or drugs) is cheaper than room and board.

The average time served on a life sentence in the United States is about six years. Murderers can usually find ways to get out of prison. So far, none has gotten out of a grave.

Charley Reese, *Conservative Chronicle*, February 15, 1989.

Clearly, life sentences do not adequately protect society, whereas the death penalty properly applied does so with certainty.

Abolitionists often cite statistics indicating that capital punishment has been administered in a discriminatory manner, so that the poor, the black, the friendless, etc., have suffered a disproportionate share of executions. Even if true, such discrimination would not be a valid reason for abandoning the death penalty unless it could be shown that it was responsible for the execution of *innocent* persons (which it has not been, to date). Most attempts to pin the "discrimination" label on capital convictions are similar to one conducted at Stanford University a few years ago, which found that murderers of white people (whether white or black) are more likely to be punished with death than are killers of black people (whether white or black). But the study also concluded that blacks who murdered whites were somewhat *less* likely to receive death sentences than were whites who killed whites. . . .

Flagrant Discrimination

The most flagrant example of discrimination in the administration of the death penalty does not involve race, income, or social status, but gender. Women commit around 13 percent of the murders in America, yet, from 1930 to June 30, 1990, only 33 of the 3991 executions (less than 1 percent) involved women. Only one of the 134 persons executed since 1976 (through July

103

18, 1990) has been a woman (Velma Barfield in North Carolina on November 2, 1984). One state governor commuted the death sentence of a woman because "humanity does not apply to women the inexorable law that it does to men."

According to L. Kay Gillespie, professor of sociology at Weber State College in Utah, evidence indicates that women who cried during their trials had a better chance of getting away with murder and avoiding the death penalty. Perhaps the National Organization for Women can do something about this glaring example of sexist "inequality" and "injustice." In the meantime, we shall continue to support the death penalty despite the disproportionate number of men who have been required to pay a just penalty for their heinous crimes. . . .

In 1953 the renowned British jurist Lord Alfred Denning asserted: "Punishment is the way in which society expresses its denunciation of wrongdoing; and in order to maintain respect for law, it is essential that the punishment for grave crimes shall adequately reflect the revulsion felt by a great majority of citizens for them." Nineteen years later, U.S. Supreme Court Justice Potter Stewart noted (while nevertheless concurring in the Court's 1972 opinion that temporarily banned capital punishment) that the "instinct for retribution is part of the nature of man and channeling that instinct in the administration of criminal justice serves an important purpose in promoting the stability of a society governed by law. When people begin to believe that organized society is unwilling or unable to impose upon criminal offenders the punishment they 'deserve,' then there are sown the seeds of anarchy—of self-help, vigilante justice, and lynch law."

Protecting the Innocent

To protect the innocent and transfer the fear and burden of crime to the criminal element where it belongs, we must demand that capital punishment be imposed when justified and expanded to cover terrible crimes in addition to murder.

"The death penalty does not work."

The Death Penalty Is Not an Effective Punishment

Matthew L. Stephens

The death penalty is arbitrary, expensive, and does nothing to prevent murder, Matthew L. Stephens contends in the following viewpoint. Stephens argues that death sentences are disproportionately applied to defendants who are poor, mentally retarded, uneducated, or members of a minority. In addition, he states that the death penalty is impractical: it is costly and does not deter crime. Stephens is a chaplain at Lebanon Correctional Institute in Ohio and the chairman of the National Interreligious Task Force on Criminal Justice, a body of the National Council of Churches of Christ.

As you read, consider the following questions:

1. What evidence does the author give to substantiate his belief that the death penalty is racist?
2. Why has the prosecution of capital punishment cases become so expensive, according to Stephens?
3. Why doesn't the author believe the death penalty deters crime?

Matthew L. Stephens, "Instrument of Justice or Tool of Vengeance?" *Christian Social Action*, November 1990. Reprinted with permission from *Christian Social Action* magazine. Copyright © 1990 by the General Board of Church and Society of the United Methodist Church.

When we look at capital punishment as an instrument of the administration of justice, we must ask: 1) Is capital punishment evenly applied to all cases of murder? 2) Will those charged in a capital punishment case have both the best lawyers and defense available to them? 3) Is the cost of carrying out the death penalty worth the money spent to execute one person? and, 4) Is capital punishment a deterrent to murder? After all, the latter is ultimately the question our society must answer. If it works, we must carry it out; if it doesn't, it is a ghastly and irrevocable error.

Applying the Death Penalty

In the United States, we experience the tragedy of over 20,000 homicides each year. These statistics are constantly increasing due to the devastating effects of drugs, racism and poverty. Yet, we choose, as a society, only 200, (or 1 percent of all murderers) to receive the ultimate punishment of death. When one looks at the criteria for selecting this nominal fraction of all murderers, the real issues come to light. Who are these people? What is their economic and racial background? What are their legal resources and representation? What is their intellectual capacity?

The facts are clear. Those on death row are the poorest of the poor. They are disproportionately "people of color": African American (40.7 percent), Hispanic (5.72 percent), Native American (1.49 percent) and Asian (0.61 percent), as compared to European/Caucasian. This means approximately 50 percent of all death row inmates are people of color in a society in which all of these populations constitute significant minorities.

Additionally, it is estimated that over one-third of all death row inmates are mentally retarded (with IQ's [intelligence quotient] of less than 70), and that nearly half are functionally illiterate.

It is these poor and oppressed children of God who become the victims of our society's anger and need for revenge. The death penalty is clearly *not* equally applied under the law, or under the more significant mandate of moral, ethical and spiritual values of a nation founded on these principles.

In a society that champions human rights and individual dignity in all of our creeds, we are far behind the rest of the so-called "civilized" western world in showing compassion to the poor and oppressed of our country. There are only two countries that still engage the death penalty as justice: South Africa and the United States. In 1990 the South African government officially put a "hold" on death sentences and executions.

There is overwhelming evidence that race is the single most important factor in choosing those who will be sentenced to death. Of the more than 3,000 people executed since 1930, nearly half were people of color. Eighty-five percent of those executed since 1977, when new death penalty statutes were passed, were punished for crimes against white victims. This is true despite the fact that the homicide rate for people of color is roughly 50 percent higher than that of the majority community.

Sojourners/CPF. Reprinted by permission.

Take, for example, the state of Ohio where 342 people have been executed since 1884. Of this number, only one white man was executed for killing a black person. In 1989, there were 100 people on death row in Ohio: 51 black men, 45 white men and 4 black women. Ohio has not executed anyone since the state reinstituted the death penalty, but the first execution will probably take place soon. Keep in mind that the minimum age for death sentencing in Ohio is 18.

The Case of Willie Darden

Consider the historic case of Willie Jasper Darden, executed March 15, 1988 in Florida's electric chair. He was 54 years old. Willie Darden was sentenced to death for the murder of a furniture store owner in Lakeland, Florida. Darden proclaimed his innocence from the moment of his arrest until the moment of his execution, over 14 years later. Significant doubt of Darden's guilt remains.

Willie Darden was tried by an all-white jury in Inverness, Florida, a county with a history of racial segregation and oppression. The prosecutor's opening remarks in the trial demonstrate the racial implications of this case:

> . . .The testimony is going to show, I think very shortly, when the trial starts, that the victims in this case were white. And of course, Mr. Darden, the defendant, is black. Can each of you tell me you can try Mr. Darden as if he was white?

Throughout the trial, the prosecutor characterized Darden as subhuman, saying such things as, "Willie Darden is an animal who should be placed on a leash." The US Supreme Court sharply criticized this misconduct, but refused to find that it unfairly influenced the trial.

In the face of evidence that those who kill whites in Florida are nearly five times more likely to be sentenced to death than those who kill blacks, the prosecution of Willie Darden becomes the story of a man who may well have been innocent, but whose protestations were overshadowed by the color of his victim and himself.

Finally, consider the case of Delbert Tibbs who went from Chicago Theological Seminary to Florida's death row. Luckily, he did not "graduate" from either. Deciding to take some time off from his studies, he hitchhiked across country. "White boys could drop out to 'find themselves,'" says Tibbs, "but nobody ever heard of a black man needing to do the same thing." His journey ended abruptly when, being in the wrong place at the wrong time, he was arrested and later convicted for the rape of a 16-year-old girl and the murder of her boyfriend in 1974. He was sentenced to death.

It was only with the assistance of the National Council of Churches Defense Fund attorneys that on appeal, his conviction was overturned on the grounds that it was not supported by the weight of the evidence. However, he was never said to be innocent of the crime. In spite of a US Supreme Court decision that he could be retried, the state decided not to reopen the case on the grounds that the police investigation of the crime was tainted from the start. The original prosecutor said, "If there is a retrial, I will appear as a witness for Mr. Tibbs." Today, Delbert Tibbs devotes his life to his family and to anti-death penalty work across the nation and around the world.

Defending the Accused

It is more than clear that race is the single-most contributing factor to one being dealt the death penalty. In combination with poverty, lack of adequate legal representation and the drive of society for vengeance, people of color are the common victims of this catharsis of hate and cycle of violence.

The quality of legal representation of indigent defendants in capital cases is of widespread concern. Most capital defendants cannot afford to pay for their own counsel and are represented by court-appointed lawyers in private practice, or by public defenders. Many times they are given inexperienced counsel, ill-equipped to handle such cases and working with severely limited resources. Many public defenders' offices are overextended with caseloads and cannot devote the time necessary to defend a capital case.

The Official Power to Kill

I have spoken my opposition to the death penalty for more than 30 years. For all that time, I have studied it, I have watched it, I have debated it, hundreds of times. I have heard all the arguments, analyzed all the evidence I could find, measured public opinion when it was opposed, when it was indifferent, when it was passionately in favor.

And always before, I have concluded the death penalty is wrong; that it lowers us all; that it is the surrender to the worst that is in us; that it uses a power—the official power to kill by execution—which has never elevated a society, never brought back a life, never inspired anything but hate.

Mario Cuomo, *New York Law Journal*, May 1, 1989.

In rural areas, lawyers handling capital cases have little or no experience in criminal law; many are ignorant of the special issues relating to capital punishment. A recent study found that capital defendants in Texas with court-appointed lawyers were more than twice as likely to receive death sentences than those who retained counsel. The trial lawyers of a number of executed prisoners were found to have spent very little time preparing the case for trial. Often, they failed to interview potentially important witnesses or to raise mitigating factors at the proper times.

A good example of this problem is the case of John Young, a black man executed in Georgia. He was convicted in 1976 of murdering three elderly people while under the influence of drugs. He was 18 years old. His trial lawyer was disbarred from legal practice within days after the trial and left the state of Georgia.

When the lawyer learned of the execution, he came forward and submitted an affidavit to the court in which he admitted spending hardly any time preparing for the case, due to personal problems. He admitted he did not investigate his client's background or raise any mitigating circumstances at the sentencing stage of the trial that might have influenced the jury's decision. These circumstances included the fact that at the age of three, John Young had seen his mother murdered while he was lying in bed with her. He later was placed with an alcoholic relative who turned him out on the street to survive at an early age. The US District Court and the Court of Appeals ruled that they could not consider the lawyer's affidavit as new evidence because it should have been presented earlier. John Young died because of inadequate defense counsel.

The Cost of Capital Punishment

Certainly there is the moral cost of taking a life, to make up for the taking of another life. There is no real way to replace one life with the death of another. Yet when capital punishment is the choice of the courts, this is exactly what has been decided.

The moral issue here is: Do we have the right to kill, or is that the right of God only? This does not excuse one who takes the life of another. That is clearly wrong. They will have to answer to the vengeance of their God. We do have the right to demand restitution and protection in the form of taking away the freedom of that individual found guilty of taking a life.

Taking freedom from individuals who kill others has also been shown to be less costly than executing them through our court system. The current debate on side-stepping a lengthy appeal process is nothing more than a rationale to expedite the death sentence while saving money.

In 1972, the Supreme Court of the United States, in *Furman vs. Georgia* held that "arbitrary and capricious" application of capital punishment violated the Eighth Amendment prohibition against cruel and unusual punishment. This means that a defendant has to be prosecuted and convicted in a way that is extraordinarily righteous and free of any kind of prejudice.

This "super" due process requirement has made the prosecutions of capital cases enormously expensive. In a University of California at Davis Law Review article, Margaret Garey calculated that it costs a minimum of $500,000 to complete a capital case in California. It costs approximately $30,000 per year to house an inmate in the California system.

Between August of 1977 and December of 1985, only 10 percent (190 of 1,847 cases) resulted in the death sentence. Data from New York State suggests that if it adopted capital punishment, the cost would be $1,828,000 per capital trial. Assuming even a 0.75 percent failure rate, it would cost about $7.3 million to sentence one person to death in New York, compared with $4.5 million ($500,000 x 0.90 percent failure rate) to sentence one person to death in California.

Cost effectiveness is a weak argument when talking about the value of human life. However, even when put on such a shallow rationale as cost-analysis, the death penalty does not hold up.

It has cost the state of Florida $57 million to execute 18 men. It is estimated that this is six times the cost of life imprisonment. A report from the *Miami Herald* said that keeping a prisoner in jail for life would cost the state $515,964 based on a 40-year life span in prison. It would cost $3.17 million for each execution. The newspaper broke the cost of execution down to show $36,000 to $116,700 for trial and sentencing; $69,480 to $160,000 for mandatory state review, which is not required in non-capital trials; $274,820 to $1 million for additional appeals; $37,600 to $312,000 for jail costs, and $845,000 for the actual execution.

A Humane Society

Moralists have traditionally acknowledged that a state may employ capital punishment if in desperate situations it has no alternatives. A country reduced to that expedient would be, however, one in which neither political intelligence nor respect for life were fully developed. On the other hand, abolition of the death penalty contributes to the common good, for it is a step toward a more humane and rational society, one that can resist violence without itself behaving violently.

America, November 12, 1988.

These figures should make us ask ourselves: Is the need for our vengeance worth all this money when the possibility that we still convict and execute the wrong person exists? What really guides our conscience—the money or the moral issue of state murder and street murder? Whatever side moves us, we must see that the cost of capital punishment is too high.

A Deterrent to Murder?

Since capital punishment has been reinstated as a legal sentence of the law, there is no proof that shows murder has declined in any of the states in which it is being used. In fact, some states show an increase in violent crimes.

People who favor the death penalty often believe it helps reduce the number of violent crimes. This may be true if the person who considers homicide would make a rational decision in anticipation of the consequences. This rarely happens because most homicides happen in the "heat of passion", anger and under the influence of drugs or alcohol.

Studies show that murder rates in states with capital punishment, such as Illinois, differ little from the states that do not have capital punishment, such as Michigan. In 1975, the year before Canada abolished the death penalty, the homicide rate was 3.09 per 100,000 persons. In 1986, that rate was down to 2.19 per 100,000 persons, the lowest in 15 years. In some states, the use of capital punishment increased the crime rate. In New York, between 1903 and 1963, executions were followed by a slight rise in the state's homicide rate.

A Need for Revenge

The recent cry for the death penalty in our country comes more from the need for revenge than for justice. The "get tough" attitude of the law enforcement community and our "kinder and gentler" government telling the nation that killing offenders will stop the rise of violence, is paradoxical. Could it be that violence begets violence? Could it be that as long as the state is killing, we are sending a message that killing is the way to solve problems?

With all of the various factors we have considered, it is clear, even to the casual observer, that the death penalty does not work. It cannot be taken back, and it is arbitrary in its application and racist in its result. People of faith must take a stand. We must choose the day when we will transform instead of kill, when we will "do justice and love mercy and walk humbly with our God" instead of perpetuating a system that is evil, barbaric, costly and ineffective.

> *"The empirical evidence is that the death penalty does deter."*

The Death Penalty Deters Murder

Steven Goldberg

Steven Goldberg is the chairman of the sociology department at City College in New York. In the following viewpoint, Goldberg writes that the death penalty can deter murder and is an effective way to protect the lives of many innocent people. He contends that those who oppose the death penalty have more concern for those sentenced to die than for the innocent victims of murder.

As you read, consider the following questions:

1. How does Goldberg refute the argument that the death penalty cannot deter because most murders are the result of emotional impulses?
2. Why does the author believe that society should use the death penalty even if it questions its deterrent effect?
3. What are the real motives of those who oppose the death penalty, in the author's view?

Steven Goldberg, "So What if the Death Penalty Deters?" *National Review*, June 30, 1989, © 1989 by National Review, Inc., 150 E. 35th St., New York, NY 10016. Reprinted by permission.

Does the threat of the death penalty deter people from murderous behavior more than the threat of imprisonment for life? We do not yet know with anything even approaching certainty whether the death penalty does or does not deter. The question is clearly empirical; and it is likely that sophisticated statistical techniques will eventually permit us an answer.

Professor Isaac Ehrlich and his colleagues, utilizing his statistical techniques, argue that there can be little doubt about the ability of the death penalty to deter. Ehrlich concludes that each additional execution prevents about seven or eight people from committing murder. All statistical arguments on the death penalty are, however, excruciatingly complex. Some critics, for example, have argued that increased likelihood of execution leads juries to convict fewer people, thereby offsetting the deterrent effect. If anything, the empirical evidence is that the death penalty *does* deter. But this is inevitably open to dispute. As a result, firm conclusions that the death penalty either does or does not deter are unwarranted and usually determined by one's psychological and moral leanings.

In academic and media circles, psychological and moral resistance to the idea of the death penalty usually leads to the assertion that it does not deter. These people's conclusion may or may not be correct, but it does not follow from the arguments they deploy:

1. *Since many murders result from emotional impulse (e.g., the angry husband who kills his wife), the death penalty could have, at best, only the slightest deterrent effect.* If the death penalty deters, it is likely that it does so through society's saying that certain acts are so unacceptable that society will kill someone who commits them. The individual internalizes the association of the act and the penalty throughout his life, constantly increasing his resistance to committing the act. Note that there is no implication here that the potential murderer consciously weighs the alternatives and decides that the crime is worth life in prison, but not death. No serious theory of deterrence claims that such rational calculation of punishment (as opposed to no rational calculation, or calculation only of the probability of getting caught) plays a role.

Potential Murderers

There is no *a priori* reason for assuming that this process is less relevant to emotional acts than rational acts; most husbands, when angry, slam doors, shout, or sulk. Neither the death penalty nor anything else deterred the husband who did murder his wife, *so the question is not what deterred the person who did murder (nothing did), but what deterred the person who didn't.* If the death penalty deters, it is, in all likelihood, primarily because it instills a psychological resistance to the act, not because it offers a rational argument against committing the act at the time that the decision is being made. In short, it is only *legislators* who calculate (or at least *should* calculate) the deterrent effect of the death penalty. Potential murderers simply act; the deterrent effect of the death penalty, if there is one, acts upon them. If it acts with sufficient strength, it prevents their becoming murderers. The legislator is the physicist studying the forces that move particles; the potential murderers are the moving particles.

Death Deters

The best evidence that the death penalty has a uniquely deterrent impact . . . is not based on statistics but is rather based on common sense and experience. Death is an awesome and awful penalty, qualitatively different from a prison term. While there is some statistical evidence indicating that it has a deterrent impact, common sense can sufficiently verify that the prospect of punishment by death does exert a restraining effect on some criminals who would otherwise commit a capital crime.

Charles E. Rice, *The New American*, June 8, 1987.

---

2. *There is no evidence that the death penalty deters*. This is simply untrue. Ehrlich's complex statistical techniques establish a real case that the death penalty deters. But here let us assume, for argument's sake, that there was no such evidence. The more important point is that there is a crucial difference between there being *no evidence* that two things are correlated and there being evidence that two things *are not* correlated. The latter means that we have good evidence that the two things are not related; the former means simply that we have no evidence on either side of the case.

Now, it is quite true that we must have some sort of evidence in order to even entertain the idea that two things are related. Our reason for not believing that tall Italian men are smarter than short Italian men is not simply that we have no direct evidence, but also because we have no informal evidence suggesting that this is true—and so we do not bother to even investigate the possibility. It is the lack of relevant informal evidence that permits us to ignore the difference between not having evidence that the hypothesis is true and having evidence that the hypothesis is not true.

But, in the case of penalties, we have an enormous amount of both informal and formal evidence—from everyday experience of socializing children and limiting adult behavior and from

115

such "experiments" as increasing the fees for parking violations—that, as a general rule, the greater a punishment, the fewer people will behave in the punished way. Thus, it is perfectly reasonable to expect that the death penalty would have a more dissuasive effect than would life imprisonment.

Imposing Death on the Innocent

Finally, nearly every popular article and a good many academic articles invoke the experience of the British with public hanging of pickpockets as proof that the death penalty does not deter. The argument sees the fact that pickpocketing continued long after the introduction of (public) hanging as demonstrating that the death penalty has no deterrent effect. It demonstrates no such thing, of course; at best, it demonstrates that not *every* pickpocket was dissuaded, a fact no one would doubt. Even if it could be shown that all practicing pickpockets continued to pick pockets at the same rate, this would still not address the more important question of whether some people who had not yet become pickpockets were dissuaded from doing so by the death penalty. I have no idea whether they were, but neither do those who deny the death penalty's effect.

3. *The death penalty will inevitably be imposed on some innocent people*. This is, of course, true. But it is also true that, *if* the death penalty deters, the number of innocent people whose lives are saved will, in all likelihood, dwarf the number of people executed—and *a fortiori*, the number wrongfully executed. Moreover, even the opponent of the death penalty who emphasizes wrongful executions is willing to sacrifice thousands of lives each year for the social advantages of motor vehicles. Realizing this, the opponent differentiates between the death penalty and the use of motor vehicles on the grounds that:

4. *In the case of the death penalty, it is the state that takes a life*. This seems to be an argument but is, in fact, merely a restatement of the basic ad-hoc moral objection to the death penalty. Therefore, it is fair to point out that those basing their opposition to the death penalty on the fact that it is the state that takes a life are, *if* the death penalty deters, maintaining their belief by sacrificing the (innocent) people who will be murdered because the death penalty is not invoked.

5. *The death penalty exchanges "real lives" (those of the executed) for "statistical lives" (those of the people who will not, if the death penalty deters and is invoked, be murdered)*. This argument is essentially a sentimental shrinking from reality. But even if one grants this dubious distinction, this defense is available only to the pure pacifist. The most justified military action makes exactly this exchange when it sacrifices many of society's young men in order to avoid a greater loss of life.

6. *If we do not know whether the death penalty deters, we should not use it.* As we have seen, *if* the death penalty deters, it deters the murder of people who are, in addition to being innocent, in all likelihood more numerous than the murderers who are executed. Thus, if society *does* invoke the death penalty on the assumption that the death penalty deters and is incorrect in this assumption, it unnecessarily accepts the deaths of a relatively small number of (nearly always guilty) individuals. On the other hand, if society refuses to invoke the death penalty on the assumption that the death penalty does *not* deter and is incorrect in *this* assumption, then it unnecessarily accepts the deaths of a relatively large number of innocent people. Consideration of this casts doubt on the intuitively plausible claim that, for as long as it is not known whether the death penalty deters, it should not be used. Supporters of the death penalty might turn this argument on its head, *viz.*: if we do not know for certain that the death penalty does *not* deter, then we are obliged to use it to save an unknown number of innocent lives.

Rewards and Punishments

Even though it is hard to know exactly how many murders that would otherwise have occurred were deterred by the threat of execution, it seems obvious that some prospective murderers, who might not have been deterred by the risk of imprisonment, will be deterred by the risk of death. After all, though we do not calculate most of the time, our behavior in general is strongly influenced by the nature of the risks we run. Were it not so, we would jump out of the window, regardless of height, when we wanted to reach street level rather than take the elevator. And we would never wait for a green light. Most of our actions are guided by the expectation of rewards and punishments, incentives and disincentives. Crimes are committed only when the perpetrators feel—wrongly or rightly—that the rewards outweigh the punishments (both divided by the risk).

Ernest van den Haag, *The World & I*, November 1989.

---

7. *The death penalty is "uncivilized."* If the death penalty deters, then, by definition, it results in a society in which there are fewer murders than there would be if the death penalty were not invoked. The opponent of the death penalty can, of course, render this fact irrelevant and immunize his argument by detaching it from deterrence altogether; he can assert that the death penalty is wrong *even if it deters*. He can, in other words, see the death penalty as analogous to torture for theft: the threat of torture would no doubt deter some people from theft, but would

still be unjustified. This is what is implied in the rejection of the death penalty on the grounds that it is "uncivilized" or that it "increases the climate of violence." Ultimately, these defenses of opposition are as invulnerable to refutation as they are incapable of persuading anyone who does not already accept their assumption that the deterrence of murders would not justify the use of the death penalty.

One might ask, however, what, precisely, are the definitions of "civilization" that see as "more civilized" a society in which *more* (innocent) people are murdered than would be the case if the society did not refuse to use the death penalty. Indeed, one might ask the opponent of the death penalty just how many innocent people he is willing to sacrifice to avoid executing the guilty.

8. *It is those who oppose the death penalty who act out of humane motives.* Motivation is irrelevant to the correctness of an empirical claim. However, since nearly every article on the subject accords to the opponent of the death penalty the right to claim a greater humanity (a right the opponent invokes with alacrity), it is worth noting there are alternative views of the opponent's motivation.

One such view is that the opponent's opposition flows not from feelings of humanity, but from the fact that the opponent can picture the murderer being executed, while he cannot picture the statistical group of innocent people who will be murdered if the death penalty deters but is not employed. The picture of the execution is capable, as the murder of the statistically expected victims is not, of eliciting guilt and fear of aggression with which the opponent cannot deal. He rationalizes his avoidance of these with feelings of humanity which bolster self-esteem and avoid awareness of his true motivation.

No Altruism

It is every bit as reasonable to see this as the opponent's motivation as it is to accept that his opposition flows from his self-proclaimed greater humanity. Like opponents of the death penalty, I too hope that the death penalty does not deter. If this proves to be the case, we will avoid the terrible choice that deterrence forces upon us. Unlike the opponents of the death penalty, however, I do not fool myself into thinking that this hope speaks well of one's character. After all, it is a hope that is willing to sacrifice the possibility of saving innocent people in order to avoid personal psychological pain. This doesn't count as altruism where I come from.

"The deterrence argument fails to justify the death penalty."

The Death Penalty Does Not Deter Murder

Stephen Nathanson

There is no substantial evidence that the death penalty deters crime, Stephen Nathanson argues in the following viewpoint. Nathanson maintains that life imprisonment is as effective a punishment as execution, and he refutes the two premises upon which the deterrence argument is based: that people fear death more than anything else, and that no other punishment is as effective as execution. The author is a professor of philosophy at Northeastern University in Boston, Massachusetts, and the author of *An Eye for an Eye? The Morality of Punishing by Death*, from which this viewpoint is excerpted.

As you read, consider the following questions:

1. What is the difference between self-defense and the death penalty, according to Nathanson?
2. Why does the author believe that the fear of death is not always the strongest fear?
3. How does Nathanson disagree with the findings of death penalty researcher Isaac Ehrlich?

One of the most powerful arguments made by death penalty supporters is based on the idea that the death penalty is a uniquely effective deterrent against murder. I want to examine the deterrence argument in order to see whether it is consistent with moral principles and whether it is supported by factual evidence.

The Moral Force of Deterrence

We have seen that although killing is generally immoral, there are certain kinds of killings which are justifiable, and one of them is killing in self-defense or in defense of others. Executing a murderer is not itself a case of killing in self-defense, but if death penalty advocates could show that the practice of executing murderers strongly resembles defensive killings in morally relevant ways, that would be an argument for including it on our list of justifiable exceptions. In other words, if there is some property possessed by defensive killings which makes these killings morally right and if executing murderers possesses this same property, then executing murderers would likewise be morally right.

When we compare executions with defensive killings, however, a problem arises immediately. A key factor in our judgment that killing in defense of oneself or others is morally justified is that the victim's life is actually saved by killing the attacker. This crucial factor is missing, however, when the death penalty is inflicted, for the victim is already dead, and the execution of his murderer will not restore him to life. It is hard to imagine that anyone would object to the death penalty if it did restore the victim's life, but we know that it does not have this effect.

Even though the execution of a particular murderer will neither prevent the death of the victim nor restore the victim to life, it might prevent other murders and thus prevent the deaths of other victims. This is the deterrence argument. Though we are powerless to restore life to the dead through executing murderers, we can prevent other murders from occurring by imposing this punishment. The death penalty, on this view, is a kind of social self-defense, an act which, like cases of individual self-defense, results in saving the lives of innocent persons. . . .

The Fear of Death

The common sense argument that death is the best deterrent rests on the belief that people fear death more than they fear anything else. If this is true, then threatening a person with death will have a greater effect on his behavior than any other threat. In particular, the threat of death is more likely to deter a person from committing murder than the threat of long term imprisonment.

Like many of the beliefs expressed in debates about the death penalty, this one has a great deal of surface plausibility, but a bit of reflection shows it to be unfounded. It is simply false that people fear their own deaths more than they fear anything else. This is not to deny that death is a significant evil, for surely it is that. Death is not the loss of one or two things that matter to us. It brings with it the loss of all experience, the termination of all personal plans and hopes, the extinction of all of our potential. Nonetheless, in spite of the genuine loss which typically comes with death, it is not true that death is feared more than anything else. . . .

Reprinted by permission of Doug Marlette and Creators Syndicate.

Indeed, when one begins to think about it, all of us risk our lives on many occasions. Mountain climbers risk their lives for thrill and adventure. Patriots risk their lives for their country. Speeding drivers risk their lives in order to get to their destinations a bit faster. Airplane passengers risk their lives in order to visit distant parts of the world, see friends, or complete business transactions. Cigarette smokers risk their lives for pleasure, relaxation, or just out of habit. If we all feared death more than anything else, we would engage in none of these activities.

But we don't fear death more than anything else. We are willing to risk death for innumerable reasons, ranging from the lofty and momentous to the vile and trivial. People who commit murder are like the rest of us in this respect. If they very much want to kill someone, they may well be willing to risk their own lives to do so. One might object that when people engage in the activities I have described, they don't expect to die. They may see that there is a risk, but they don't really expect death to result from their actions. If they really expected to die as a result of their actions, they would not engage in them. The lesson to be learned, according to this objection, is that if we could administer the death penalty effectively, then prospective murderers would know that if they choose to kill, their own deaths would result. If the death penalty were properly administered and potential murderers faced the certainty of their own deaths rather than a minimal risk of dying, then they would refrain from killing.

The problem with this objection is that we cannot guarantee that all murderers will be executed. Some will not be found out. Some will be tried but acquitted. Some will be found guilty of lesser charges. Some will have their sentences commuted or reversed on appeal. At best, we can increase the probability that murderers will be executed, but it is mere fantasy to expect that we can make execution certain. The result is that someone who wants to kill will be faced with the *risk* of death and not the certainty of death. There is no way that we can transform this risk into a certainty. Like the rest of us, prospective murderers will often choose to take that risk.

Lesser Punishments

It is worth noting, too, that even if people did fear death more than anything else, that would not establish that death was necessary for deterring people from committing murder. Lesser punishments might be feared enough to have the desired deterrent effect. All of us fear ten years in prison more than one year in prison, but the threat of a one year prison sentence would be quite enough to deter us from parking meter violations. The extra severity is unnecessary for insuring adequate compliance. Likewise, for most of us, the prospect of life imprisonment (or even five or ten years in prison) is so dreadful that increasing the penalty for murder from life imprisonment to death would not provide any additional discouragement. Even if death is more feared than imprisonment, it might well be that long-term imprisonment would deter as well as death. The added severity might not save additional lives.

We can see, then, that the deterrence argument based on the "common-sense" belief that people fear death more than anything else fails. It fails because it does not show either that the threat of death is sufficient to deter murders or that it is necessary to deter murders. What is surprising about the argument is that one continues to hear it and that people take it as obvious, in spite of the fact that it is inconsistent with so much of what we know about our own behavior and the behavior of others around us.

Again, none of this should suggest that death is not a great evil for most of us. It is a significant evil, but for a variety of reasons, we frequently do not take seriously the risks involved in our actions, and this results in our not being deterred from acting in ways which make death more likely. . . .

Systematic Studies of Deterrence

In trying to estimate the deterrent force of the death penalty, as compared with other punishments, one might decide to leave behind assumptions about psychological motivation and try to examine instead the actual effects of imposing or not imposing the death penalty. If proponents of the deterrence argument are correct that the death penalty reduces killings and therefore saves lives, then it is reasonable to expect that fewer people will be murdered in areas where the death penalty has been adopted and that more people will be murdered in areas where there is no death penalty. We can test the deterrent argument, then, by seeing whether more murders occur when people face the possibility of life imprisonment as the maximum sentence and whether fewer murders occur when people are threatened with the possibility of execution. . . .

Ehrlich's Analysis

The recent focus of discussion and controversy has been the work of Isaac Ehrlich.

Ehrlich is an economist whose application of techniques of economic analysis to the death penalty problem led him to conclude that each execution might be responsible for the prevention of eight deaths by murder. . . .

Ehrlich's formula represents the homicide rate as a function of several factors: the probability of a murderer being caught, the probability of his being convicted if he is caught, the probability of his being executed if he is convicted, the unemployment rate, the percentage of adults employed, per capita income levels, and the proportion of the population between fourteen and twenty-four years old. Through statistical analysis, Ehrlich thought he could pin down just how much the homicide rate was affected by the probability of execution. He concluded that there was a significant effect—about eight murders were prevented by each execution. . . .

It is clear that if Ehrlich was to succeed in measuring the effect of executions, he needed to identify correctly the main variables that affect the homicide rate and then use statistical techniques to isolate the amount of the effect due to any single variable. His result would not hold if he failed to include variables which significantly affect homicide rates. David Baldus and

James Cole argue that Ehrlich did omit important variables, citing such factors as the rate of migration from rural to urban areas, the rate of weapons ownership among the population, and the rate at which violent crimes other than murder were occurring. Since it is plausible to believe that these factors influence the homicide rate and since Ehrlich's formula omitted them, his analysis could make it appear that changes in the homicide rate were caused by executions when in fact they resulted from these omitted variables. . . .

In addition, Ehrlich studied the number of executions and homicides for the United States as a whole, rather than focusing on particular states or regions. This means that if there were significant variations among different regions, these would not be revealed by Ehrlich's study. To take an extreme case, if homicide rates had gone down drastically in non-death penalty states and risen sharply in death penalty states, Ehrlich's figures would not reveal this. Both his data and his conclusions deal only with the overall rate for the entire United States. For his results to stand up, they need to be corroborated by studies of smaller units. Peter Passell carried out state-by-state analyses of the relationship between executions and homicide rates, using methods similar to Ehrlich's. Analyzing data on forty-one states in 1950 and forty-four states in 1960, he found no deterrent effect of the sort Ehrlich claimed exists.

A final powerful criticism of Ehrlich's finding is that although his study covers a long period of time, 1932-1970, the apparent deterrent force of the death penalty emerges only as a result of homicide and execution rates after 1962. In other words, if one considers only the period up to 1962, Ehrlich's striking result does not emerge. One would think that if the death penalty exercised a steady influence on homicides, then there would be no difference if a few years were dropped from the sample, yet this is not so. The omission of the years from 1962 to 1970 has a drastic effect on Ehrlich's result.

Moreover, it is easy to account for the change which occurs after 1962. Starting at that point, the attack on capital punishment in the courts was leading to a radical drop in the number of executions. Likewise, beginning in 1965, there was a tremendous surge in the homicide rate. The result is that murders increased while executions decreased. This set of events in the 1960s is responsible for most of the effect which Ehrlich's analysis purports to find operating through the earlier decades.

Special Deterrence

These criticisms strike me as being quite forceful and, in my judgment, they effectively undermine Ehrlich's alleged vindication of the superior deterrent force of the death penalty. . . .

Before concluding, we should turn briefly to another kind of deterrence argument. The argument we have so far considered involves "general deterrence," the idea that by punishing one person, we discourage others from committing crimes. Some arguments, however, focus on "special deterrence," preventing a person who has already violated the law from committing additional crimes. Sometimes this effect of punishment is called "incapacitation."

No Justification for Death

Perhaps the most harmful cost of the death penalty results from the false assumption that it helps to fight crime. Although the death penalty has no effect on reducing the crime rate, many politicians advocate executions to show they are taking steps to make America safer. This empty gesture distracts society's attention from the difficult challenge of finding effective solutions to the very real problem of violence. Often people who favor the death penalty don't have facts. They would like to believe this punishment is justified by reason, when in fact it results only from helplessness and rage.

John G. Healey, *The World & I*, November 1989.

According to the special deterrence argument for the death penalty, we ought to execute a person who commits murder because that is the surest way of preventing that person from murdering again.

This argument rests on a proposition that no one would deny: Murderers who have been executed will not commit additional murders. The truth of this statement, however, is not enough to make the argument succeed. As we noted earlier, the analogy with killing in self-defense requires that killing to save lives is justified only if there is no less severe action which would have the same effect. In this case, however, life imprisonment would provide the same protection to society that execution does. It would isolate convicted murderers and thus deprive them of further opportunities to kill innocent citizens. . . .

Conclusions

I believe that there is a basis for a confident rejection of the deterrence thesis, but even the more cautious and limited conclusion that the deterrent effect has not been proved is sufficient for undermining the deterrence argument. The death penalty can be justified as analogous to defensive killing only if it can be shown that it does save lives. Since that has not been shown, one cannot appeal to this protective function as providing a moral basis for executing murderers. Despite the initial moral force of the deterrence argument, its factual presupposition—that the death penalty saves lives—is not sufficiently supported by available evidence. The deterrence argument fails to justify the death penalty.

"States seeking to carry out the [death] sentence . . . should not have to wait eight years to do that."

Limitless Appeals Make the Death Penalty Ineffective

William H. Rehnquist

Many death penalty supporters have suggested that a limit be placed on the number of times a defendant may appeal the death sentence. In 1989, a committee headed by former United States Supreme Court Justice Lewis F. Powell Jr. recommended such limits to Congress. In the following viewpoint, Supreme Court Chief Justice William H. Rehnquist supports the Powell committee's recommendations. Rehnquist believes limiting the number of appeals would improve the efficiency of the court system and improve the quality of justice in the nation. Rehnquist, appointed chief justice in 1986, has served on the Supreme Court since 1972.

As you read, consider the following questions:

1. What does Rehnquist state should be the goal of court review procedures?
2. How does the appeals process differ in the civil and criminal courts, according to the author?
3. Why does Rehnquist think the Powell committee's recommendations would improve the court system?

William H. Rehnquist, from a speech delivered to the American Law Institute, Philadelphia, PA, May 15, 1990.

Today we have a serious malfunction in our legal system—the manner in which death sentences imposed by state courts are reviewed in the federal courts. Today the average length of time between the date on which a trial court imposes a sentence of death, and the date that sentence is carried out—after combined state and federal review of the sentence—is between seven and eight years. More than three years of this time are taken up by collateral review alone, with little certainty as to when that review has run its course.

Surely a judicial system properly designed to consider both the claim of the state to have its laws enforced and the claim of the defendant to the protections guaranteed him by the federal Constitution should be able to reach a final decision in less time than this.

The essence of the question is not the pros and cons of capital punishment, but the pros and cons of federalism. The Supreme Court has held that capital punishment is lawful if imposed consistently with the requirements of the Eighth Amendment. Whether or not a state should choose to have capital punishment must be up to each state: thirty-seven states have elected to have it, and thirteen states have chosen not to have it. The capital punishment question is one which deeply divides people, and always has. But this question is only tangentially involved when we consider the procedures designed to provide collateral review in the federal courts for federal constitutional claims of defendants who have been sentenced to death. Surely the goal must be to allow the states to carry out a lawful capital sentence, while at the same time assuring the capital defendant meaningful review of the lawfulness of his sentence under the federal Constitution in the federal courts. This, as I have said, is essentially a question of federalism—what is the proper balance between the lawful authority of the states and the role of federal courts in protecting constitutional rights?

The Writ of Habeas Corpus

The writ of habeas corpus was originally a creature of the English common law, not designed to challenge judgments of conviction rendered after trial, but to challenge unlawful detention of citizens by the executive. It played much the same role in this country for the first century and a half of our existence. As a result of judicial decisions and congressional ratification of these decisions over the past century, however, it has evolved into something quite different. In civil litigation, as we all know, once the parties have had a trial and whatever appeals are available, the litigation comes to an end and the judgment is final. But in criminal cases a defendant whose conviction has become final on direct review in the state courts may nonetheless raise federal constitutional objections to that conviction and sentence in a federal habeas proceeding. This system is unique to the United States; no such collateral attack is allowed on a criminal conviction in England where the writ of habeas corpus originated.

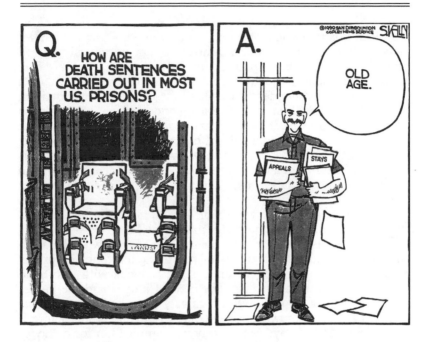

© Steve Kelley/Copley News Service. Reprinted with permission.

Reasonable people have questioned whether a criminal defendant ought to have as broad a "second bite at the apple" in the federal courts as he presently does, but that is a question of policy for Congress to decide. So long as we are speaking of noncapital defendants, the present system does not present the sort of practical difficulties in the administration of justice that it presents in the case of capital defendants. This is because someone who is convicted and sentenced to prison for a term of years in state court, and wishes to challenge that conviction and sentence in a federal habeas proceeding, has every incentive to move promptly to make that challenge. He must continue to serve his sentence while his federal claims are being adjudicated in the federal courts. Therefore, the sooner he obtains a decision on these claims, the sooner he will get the benefit of any decision that is favorable to him. This is true even though there is no statute of limitations for bringing the federal habeas proceeding.

But the incentives are quite the other way with a capital defendant. All federal review of his sentence must obviously take place *before* the sentence is carried out; consequently, the capital defendant frequently finds it in his interest to do nothing until a death warrant is actually issued by the state.

Additional Stays

Not only is there no statute of limitations for filing for federal habeas, but . . . a criminal defendant is not necessarily barred from bringing a second petition in federal court after his first petition has been decided against him on the merits. . . . As a result, a capital defendant, after his first federal habeas petition is decided against him, may file a second petition, and even on occasion a third petition. On each occasion, arguments are pressed that an additional stay of execution is required in order for a court to consider these successive petitions. The result is that at no point until a death sentence is actually carried out can it be said that litigation concerning the sentence has run its course.

The system at present verges on the chaotic. The eight years between conviction in the state court and final decision in the federal courts is consumed not by structured review of the arguments of the parties, but in fits of frantic action followed by periods of inaction. My colleagues and I can speak with first hand experience of this, and so can the district judges and the judges of the courts of appeals who regularly pass on these applications. It is not unknown for our court to have pending before it within a period of days not merely one application for a stay of execution but two from the same person: one seeking review of collateral state proceedings, and the other seeking review of federal habeas proceedings, both brought in the court of first instance within a matter of days before the execution is set to take place. Thus delay is not the only fault in the present system. The last-minute nature of so many of the proceedings in both the state courts and the federal courts leaves one with little sense that the legal process has run an orderly course, whether a stay is granted or whether it is denied. . . .

This system cries out for reform. I submit that no one—whether favorable to the prosecution, favorable to the defense, or somewhere in between—would ever have consciously designed it. The question is how the present law can be changed to deal with these problems while still serving the federalism goal which I mentioned previously.

The Powell Committee

In June 1988 I established an Ad Hoc Committee on Federal Habeas Corpus in Capital Cases under the chairmanship of retired Associate Justice Lewis F. Powell, Jr. . . .

The Committee investigated ways of improving both the fairness and efficiency of our system of collateral review in death penalty cases. In September of 1989 it issued its report recommending the coordination of our state and federal legal systems in capital cases and the structuring of collateral review. The Report concluded that capital cases "should be subject to one fair and complete course of collateral review in the state and federal system, free from time pressure of impending execution and with the assistance of competent counsel."

Under the Powell Committee proposal, persons convicted of capital crimes and sentenced to death would, after a full set of appeals, have one opportunity to collaterally attack their sentences at the state level and one such opportunity at the federal level. Second and successive petitions for collateral review would be entertained only if the petitioner could cast doubt upon the legitimacy of his conviction of a capital crime. In the absence of underlying doubt concerning guilt or innocence, itself, courts would not entertain repetitive petitions attacking the appropriateness of the death sentence. . . .

I believe that the Powell Committee Report strikes a sound balance between the need for ensuring a careful review in the federal courts of a capital defendant's constitutional claims and the need for the state to carry out the sentence once the federal courts have determined that its imposition was consistent with federal law. . . .

Reforming the System

At this moment, there are about twenty-two hundred capital defendants on the various "death rows" in state prisons. There is no doubt that when some of these defendants present their constitutional claims to federal courts, their sentences will be set aside. Others of these defendants will, after full federal review, obtain a determination that the sentences imposed on them were consistent with the federal Constitution. Defendants who will ultimately prevail in their claims should not have to wait eight years for a decision to that effect, and states seeking to carry out the sentence upon defendants whose claims are rejected by federal courts should not have to wait eight years to do that. Fair-minded people, whether they personally oppose or favor the death penalty, should have no difficulty agreeing that the present system is badly in need of reform. . . .

The proposal of the Powell Committee, in my view, accomplishes the task while the others do not. Under that proposal the capital defendant is given the necessary tools and the necessary incentives to make all of his constitutional claims in his first federal habeas proceeding, and that proceeding is allowed to run its full course in both the district court and in the court of appeals without any threat of imminent execution. If the result of

131

these proceedings is a determination that the state sentence is consistent with the United States Constitution, that should (with rare exceptions) conclude the federal review, and the state should be able to carry out its sentence. This is a solution to the problem in the best tradition of our federal system. It is a solution which will restore public confidence in the way capital punishment is imposed and carried out in our country.

"We must not deprive any human being of a fair chance for judicial review."

Limiting Death Sentence Appeals Would Harm Civil Rights

Stephen Reinhardt

The Powell committee, headed by former U.S. Supreme Court Justice Lewis F. Powell Jr., recommended that Congress limit the number of appeals for those sentenced to die. In the following viewpoint, Stephen Reinhardt argues that such measures would threaten the constitutional rights of many defendants, would increase the number of executions, and would threaten the lives of innocent people wrongly sentenced to die. Reinhardt states that as long as courts, juries, and judges remain fallible, defendants should be allowed as many appeals as are necessary to ensure that justice is done. The author is a judge on the United States Court of Appeals for the Ninth Circuit.

As you read, consider the following questions:

1. What example does Reinhardt give to show how federal review and the writ of habeas corpus protect defendants?
2. Why does the author believe that both supporters and opponents of the death penalty should oppose limiting a defendant's right to appeal?
3. What will be the effect of the Powell committee recommendations, in the author's opinion?

Stephen Reinhardt, "Must We Rush the Executioner?" *Los Angeles Times*, November 7, 1989. Reprinted with permission.

A committee headed by former Supreme Court Justice Lewis F. Powell Jr. and composed exclusively of federal judges from the South has recommended drastic limitations on the rights of condemned people awaiting execution. In California alone, there are more than 200 who may be affected by these changes in our fundamental procedures.

The Powell committee report, which Chief Justice William Rehnquist submitted directly to Congress in a manner that drew unprecedented criticism from most of the chief judges of the U.S. Courts of Appeal, would severely restrict the use of the writ of habeas corpus in capital cases. Speedy executions, rather than fairness and due process, would be the order of the day.

Are we really so desperate to execute people that we can no longer afford them the full rights of review that condemned people have always had? Are we really willing to sacrifice certainty for speed where life is at stake? Are we really prepared to execute people who have been convicted or sentenced in violation of the provisions of the Constitution?

If not, someone had better tell the Congress before it enacts the Powell committee recommendations. Legislation that would accomplish just that is now on a special fast track, which would permit Congress to act before the lessons of common sense and history can make their weight felt.

Fundamental Violations

The issue is not, as some seem to believe, whether we should turn criminals loose simply because courts make technical errors or admit improper evidence. It is whether in capital cases we can afford to ignore fundamental constitutional violations that may affect the jury's decision to find the defendant guilty or to impose a death sentence instead of life imprisonment.

If the error is not of constitutional magnitude or if it does not affect the verdict, the federal courts will not intervene.

The writ of habeas corpus, no less, is under attack by the chief justice and the committee he appointed. One might expect to hear the alarm bells ringing throughout the land. Yet only the American Bar Assn. has thus far shown any signs of springing into action. Its litigation section has issued a report calling for greater, rather than lesser, protections for the rights of those facing death at the hands of the state. . . .

To understand the significance of these attempts to limit federal-court review of state-imposed death sentences, one need only look back over a recent seven-year period. During that time, almost 75% of the orders of execution issued by state courts were found to be in violation of the Constitution. But for federal review and the writ of habeas corpus, a substantial number of people would have been executed in contravention of the fundamental principles set forth in our Bill of Rights.

In some cases, the defendant may have been innocent; in others, only the fairness of the sentence may have been at issue. Either way, the lesson is simple: Courts make mistakes—even in capital cases. And they make them more frequently than we like to admit. This elementary fact should lead us all, supporters and opponents of the death penalty alike, to one uncontroversial conclusion: We must be absolutely sure that we are right before we drop the pellet or pull the switch. We must not deprive any human being of a fair chance for judicial review if a reasonable argument exists that reversal of his or her death penalty is required by our laws.

No Shortcuts

According to the old adage: "justice delayed is justice denied." Yet when it comes to the death penalty, an inordinate amount of time elapses between arrest and trial and between the imposition of a death sentence and any execution. This causes the public to question whether all of the "delay" is necessary.

I don't believe there are any shortcuts. The severity and finality of the penalty dictates the nature and speed of the process which must be followed before any execution can take place. . . .

Some would argue that those convicted of heinous crimes don't deserve constitutional rights or should forfeit them. But rights only have meaning if they can be relied on by the weak or those we may despise. The right to free speech, for example, would be quite meaningless if we limited it to those whose words we wanted to hear.

So long as we have a Constitution that values due process and so long as we have an adversarial system, any attempt to impose capital punishment will take time.

Jan Stiglitz, *The San Diego Union*, May 6, 1990.

This is the very principle that the Powell committee squarely and explicitly rejects. The committee's recommendations reflect an understandable public frustration over increasing crime, the narcotics threat, the slowness of the judicial process and our general inability to control our national and individual destinies. We want to strike out—to act—to see tangible results, at last.

A Simplistic Solution

What is more tangible and final than an execution? And what is more difficult to understand than why it takes the courts so long to decide that a mass murderer should be executed? So, the

Powell committee looked for ways to speed up the death-penalty process. And it found a simplistic solution. Limit the use of the historic writ of habeas corpus in capital cases. Afford condemned prisoners fewer rights than persons convicted of lesser offenses. Prohibit successive habeas petitions in capital cases, unlike in all other felonies. Adopt a rule that if a capital prisoner's lawyer fails to raise an issue in the state proceedings, the prisoner is barred from ever raising it in federal court. Adopt another rule that any issue not raised the first time the case is presented to a federal judge is, except in rare instances, forever waived.

These rules might be helpful and reasonable if all lawyers were perfect. But lawyers, like judges, are not. Lawyers make mistakes, too. And the Powell committee's view is that it is the condemned man (or woman) who should pay for those mistakes—with their lives.

The Powell committee's report is not entirely without redeeming social value. For example, it encourages states to adopt procedures for the appointment of counsel for indigents who want to file habeas petitions in capital cases.

Unconstitutional Procedures

On the other hand, it reaffirms the rule that prohibits condemned prisoners from asserting constitutional rights that the Supreme Court had not acknowledged as of the time the crime was committed. How much fairer and more sensible the view of the bar association committee: "We believe it is unacceptable to sanction executions under procedures that have been declared unconstitutional."

The Powell committee met only six times. It was composed exclusively of judges from places in which executions are common. It heard from no witnesses, accepting only written comments. Yet it felt sufficiently confident of its views to recommend the most radical curtailment of the writ of habeas corpus in our history.

It may take years before all the consequences surrounding adoption of the Powell committee recommendations become evident. Meanwhile, executions will certainly increase—but at what cost to our Constitution?

a critical thinking activity

Distinguishing Between Fact and Opinion

This activity is designed to help develop the basic reading and thinking skill of distinguishing between fact and opinion. Consider the following statement: "It has cost Florida $57 million to execute eighteen men." This is a factual statement because it could be checked by looking at statistics from Florida's state government. But the statement "The cost of capital punishment is too high" is an opinion. Many death penalty advocates believe that the benefits of the death penalty outweigh the costs.

When investigating controversial issues it is important that one be able to distinguish between statements of fact and statements of opinion. It is also important to recognize that not all statements of fact are true. They may appear to be true, but some are based on inaccurate or false information. For this activity, however, we are concerned with understanding the difference between those statements which appear to be factual and those which appear to be based primarily on opinion.

Most of the following statements are taken from the viewpoints in this chapter. Consider each statement carefully. *Mark O for any statement you believe is an opinion or interpretation of facts. Mark F for any statement you believe is a fact. Mark I for any statement you believe is impossible to judge.*

If you are doing this activity as a member of a class or group, compare your answers with those of other class or group members. Be able to defend your answers. You may discover that others come to different conclusions than you do. Listening to the reasons others present for their answers may give you valuable insights into distinguishing between fact and opinion.

O = *opinion*
F = *fact*
I = *impossible to judge*

1. The average length of time between the imposition of a death sentence and the execution of the criminal is eight years.

2. Deterrence should never be considered the primary reason for administering the death penalty.

3. Life imprisonment is a flawed alternative to the death penalty.

4. Cost effectiveness is a weak argument when talking about the value of a human life.

5. According to the Department of Justice, it costs around $20,000 a year to house a prisoner.

6. Capital punishment causes an increase in violent crime.

7. Some prospective murderers will be deterred by the risk of death.

8. In New York between 1903 and 1963, executions were followed by a rise in the state's homicide rate.

9. Isaac Ehrlich concluded from his research that every execution prevents about eight murders.

10. The average time served on a life sentence in the United States is about six years.

11. Due to costly delays and endless appeals, the death penalty has been made ineffective.

12. There are only two Western countries that still use the death penalty: the United States and South Africa.

13. Abolition of the death penalty contributes to the common good.

14. Approximately three-fourths of the American people favor capital punishment.

15. The death penalty has no effect on reducing the crime rate.

16. The death penalty never inspired anything but hate.

17. Some defendants who have been executed were later found to be innocent.

18. The exorbitant financial expense of death penalty cases is regularly cited by abolitionists as a reason for abolishing capital punishment.

Periodical Bibliography

The following articles have been selected to supplement the diverse views presented in this chapter.

Charlotte Low Allen	"Ending Abuse of Death Penalty Appeals," *The Wall Street Journal*, May 14, 1990.
Amnesty International	*The Death Penalty: Cruel and Unusual Punishment*. Available from 322 Eighth Ave., New York, NY 10001.
Sharon Begley	"The Slow Pace on Death Row," *Newsweek*, February 8, 1988.
William F. Buckley Jr.	"The War Against Capital Punishment," *National Review*, June 25, 1990.
Jason DeParle	"The Juice Ain't No Use," *The Washington Monthly*, May 1989.
Don Feder	"Without the Death Sentence, Innocents Die," *Conservative Chronicle*, January 31, 1990. Available from PO Box 11297, Des Moines, IA 50340-1297.
Tom Gibbons	"Victims Again: Survivors Suffer Through Capital Appeals," *ABA Journal*, September 1, 1988. Available from the American Bar Association, 750 N. Lake Shore Dr., Chicago, IL 60611.
Linda Greenhouse	"The Court Cuts Off Another Exit from Death Row," *The New York Times*, March 11, 1990.
David A. Kaplan	"Killing the Rights of the Condemned," *The New York Times*, June 27, 1990.
Leo Pfeffer	"The Death Penalty and American Jewry," *The Humanist*, January/February 1991.
Charles E. Rice	"Capital Punishment: An Examination of Its Purpose in Serving Justice," *The New American*, June 8, 1987. Available from The Review of the News Incorporated, 770 Westhill Blvd., Appleton, WI 54915.
Ted Rohrlich	"Does Death Penalty Deter Killers? No Clear Answer," *Los Angeles Times*, March 23, 1990.
Scientific American	"The Death Penalty: Most Americans Favor It, but What Purpose Does It Serve?" July 1990.
John Wilkes	"Murder in Mind," *Psychology Today*, June 1987.

Does the Death Penalty Discriminate?

Chapter Preface

Throughout America's history, the death penalty has been applied disproportionately to the poor and to minorities. For example, of the 455 criminals executed for rape after 1930 in southern states, 405 were black. The U.S. Supreme Court in 1972 recognized this discrimination when it ruled in *Furman v. Georgia* that courts were applying the death penalty arbitrarily, in violation of the Eighth and Fourteenth Amendments. Justice William O. Douglas stated:

The discretion of judges and juries in imposing the death penalty enables the penalty to be selectively applied, feeding prejudices against the accused if he is poor and despised and lacks political clout, or if he is a member of a suspect or unpopular minority.

This ruling, in essence, stopped all executions for several years. States, fearing that the Supreme Court would overturn death sentences on the basis of discrimination, temporarily discontinued executions and scurried to revise and reintroduce their death penalty statutes. By 1975, thirty-three states had revised their statutes, enabling them once again to execute criminals.

At first, most legal experts applauded these changes and believed that they would reduce discriminatory capital sentencing. Now, however, some experts assert that these revisions and precautions have done little to curtail discrimination, and they argue that nearly 50 percent of the defendants on death row are black and nearly all of them are poor. In contrast, only about 12 percent of the general population is black and only about 14 percent is poor. A 1990 Government Accounting Office report found "racial disparities in charging, sentencing, and the imposition of the death penalty."

Other legal experts, however, believe that the state revisions after *Furman* greatly reduced discrimination in death penalty sentencing. They maintain that since 46 percent of prison inmates are black and a large percentage of criminals are poor, the percentage of blacks and the poor receiving the death sentence will be much higher than the percentage of blacks and poor in the overall population. "It is simply an unhappy fact that blacks commit a disproportionate number of the known crimes in the United States," writes Walter Berns, author of *For Capital Punishment: Crime and the Morality of the Death Penalty*. He continues, "To execute black murderers or poor murderers because they are murderers is not unjust."

The authors in the following chapter debate whether the death penalty discriminates.

"Black defendants . . . have always been sentenced to death and executed far out of proportion to their numbers."

The Death Penalty Discriminates Against Blacks

Anthony G. Amsterdam

Anthony G. Amsterdam is a law professor at New York University Law School in New York City. In the following viewpoint, Amsterdam asserts that blacks are much more likely than whites to be sentenced to death, and that murderers whose victims were white are more likely to receive the death sentence than those whose victims were black. The author believes these discrepancies are the result of racism.

As you read, consider the following questions:

1. Why does the author believe the McCleskey case is important?
2. How does the Baldus study prove that the death penalty is racist, in Amsterdam's opinion?
3. Why does Amsterdam believe the U.S. Supreme Court ruled against McCleskey?

Anthony G. Amsterdam, "Race and the Death Penalty." Reprinted, with permission of the Institute for Criminal Justice Ethics, from *Criminal Justice Ethics*, vol. 7, no. 1 (Winter/Spring 1988), pp. 2, 84-86.

There are times when even truths we hold self-evident require affirmation. For those who have invested our careers and our hopes in the criminal justice system, this is one of those times. Insofar as the basic principles that give value to our lives are in the keeping of the law and can be vindicated or betrayed by the decisions of any court, they have been sold down the river by a decision of the Supreme Court of the United States.

I do not choose by accident a metaphor of slavery. For the decision I am referring to is the criminal justice system's *Dred Scott* case. It is the case of Warren McCleskey, a black man sentenced to die for the murder of a white man in Georgia. The Supreme Court held that McCleskey can be constitutionally put to death despite overwhelming unrebutted and unexplained statistical evidence that the death penalty is being imposed by Georgia juries in a pattern which reflects the race of convicted murderers and their victims and cannot be accounted for by any factor other than race. . . .

The McCleskey Case

Let us look at the *McCleskey* case. His crime was an ugly one. He robbed a furniture store at gunpoint, and he or one of his accomplices killed a police officer who responded to the scene. McCleskey may have been the triggerman. Whether or not he was, he was guilty of murder under Georgia law.

But his case in the Supreme Court was not concerned with guilt. It was concerned with why McCleskey had been sentenced to death instead of life imprisonment for his crime. It was concerned with why, out of seventeen defendants charged with the killings of police officers in Fulton County, Georgia, between 1973 and 1980, only Warren McCleskey—a black defendant charged with killing a white officer—had been chosen for a death sentence. In the only other one of these seventeen cases in which the predominantly white prosecutor's office in Atlanta had pushed for the death penalty, a black defendant convicted of killing a black police officer had been sentenced to life instead.

It was facts of that sort that led the NAACP [National Association for the Advancement of Colored People] Legal Defense Fund to become involved in McCleskey's case. They were not unfamiliar facts to any of the lawyers who, like myself, had worked for the Legal Defense Fund for many years, defending Blacks charged with serious crimes throughout the South. We knew that in the United States black defendants convicted of murder or rape in cases involving white victims have always been sentenced to death and executed far out of proportion to their numbers, and under factual circumstances that would have produced a sentence of imprisonment—often a relatively light sentence of imprisonment—in identical cases with black victims or white defendants or both. . . .

The evidence that we presented in support of McCleskey's claim of racial discrimination left nothing out. Our centerpiece was a pair of studies conducted by Professor David Baldus, of the University of Iowa, and his colleagues, which examined 2,484 cases of murder and non-negligent manslaughter that occurred in Georgia between 1973, the date when its present capital murder statute was enacted, and 1979, the year after McCleskey's own death sentence was imposed. . . .

Reprinted by permission of Doug Marlette and Creators Syndicate.

The Baldus study has since been uniformly praised by social scientists as the best study of any aspect of criminal sentencing ever conducted.

What did it show? That death sentences were being imposed in Georgia murder cases in a clear, consistent pattern that reflected the race of the victim and the race of the defendant and could not be explained by any non-racial factor. For example:

(1) Although less than 40 percent of Georgia homicide cases involve white victims, in 87 percent of the cases in which a death sentence is imposed, the victim is white. White-victim cases are almost eleven times more likely to produce a death sentence than are black-victim cases.

144

(2) When the race of the defendant is considered too, the following figures emerge: 22 percent of black defendants who kill white victims are sentenced to death; 8 percent of white defendants who kill white victims are sentenced to death; 1 percent of black defendants who kill black victims are sentenced to death; 3 percent of white defendants who kill black victims are sentenced to death. It should be noted that out of the roughly 2,500 Georgia homicide cases found, only 64 involved killings of black victims by white defendants, so the 3 percent death-sentencing rate in this category represents a total of two death sentences over a six-year period. Plainly, the reason why racial discrimination against black defendants does not appear even more glaringly evident is that most black murderers kill black victims; almost no identified white murderers kill black victims; and virtually nobody is sentenced to death for killing a mere black victim.

(3) No non-racial factor explains these racial patterns. Under multiple regression analysis, the model with the maximum explanatory power shows that after controlling for legitimate non-racial factors, murderers of white victims are still being sentenced to death 4.3 times more often than murderers of black victims. Multiple regression analysis also shows that the race of the victim is as good a basis for predicting whether or not a murderer will be sentenced to death as are the aggravating circumstances which the Georgia statute explicitly says should be considered in favor of a death sentence, such as whether the defendant has a prior murder conviction, or whether he is the primary actor in the present murder.

(4) Across the whole universe of cases, approximately 5 percent of Georgia killings result in a death sentence. Yet when more than 230 non-racial variables are controlled for, the death-sentencing rate is 6 percentage points higher in white-victim cases than in black-victim cases. What this means is that in predicting whether any particular person will get the death penalty in Georgia, it is less important to know whether or not he committed a homicide in the first place than to know whether, if he did, he killed a white victim or a black one.

The Severity of the Crime

(5) However, the effects of race are not uniform across the entire range of homicide cases. As might be expected, in the least aggravated sorts of cases, almost no one gets a death sentence; in the really gruesome cases, a high percentage of both black and white murderers get death sentences; so it is in the mid-range of cases—cases like McCleskey's—that race has its greatest impact. The Baldus study found that in these mid-range cases the death-sentencing rate for killers of white victims is 34

145

percent as compared to 14 percent for killers of black victims. In other words, out of every thirty-four murderers sentenced to death for killing a white victim, twenty of them would not have gotten death sentences if their victims had been black.

A Violation of Human Rights

The death penalty violates the most basic of human rights, the right to live, of mainly Afro-Americans and working people. In this regard we should not overlook the fact that our government is violating international law and internationally accepted democratic norms. For 48 per cent of the death row population in our country to be Black is clearly practicing genocide when you consider that Afro-Americans are only 12 per cent of the population.

Frank Chapman, *Political Affairs*, July 1987.

The bottom line is this: Georgia has executed eleven murderers since it passed its present statute in 1973. Nine of the eleven were black. Ten of the eleven had white victims. Can there be the slightest doubt that this revolting record is the product of some sort of racial bias rather than a pure fluke?

A narrow majority of the Supreme Court pretended to have such doubts and rejected McCleskey's Equal-Protection challenge to his death sentence. It did not question the quality or the validity of the Baldus study, or any of the findings that have been described here. It admitted that the manifest racial discrepancies in death sentencing were unexplained by any nonracial variable, and that Baldus's data pointed to a "likelihood" or a "risk" that race was at work in the capital sentencing process. It essentially conceded that if a similar statistical showing of racial bias had been made in an employment-discrimination case or in a jury-selection case, the courts would have been required to find a violation of the Equal Protection Clause of the Fourteenth Amendment. But, the Court said, racial discrimination in capital sentencing cannot be proved by a pattern of sentencing results: a death-sentenced defendant like McCleskey must present proof that the particular jury or the individual prosecutor, or some other decision-maker in his own case, was personally motivated by racial considerations to bring about his death. Since such proof is never possible to obtain, racial discrimination in capital sentencing is never possible to prove. . . .

No Justice

What the Supreme Court has held, plainly, is that the very nature of the criminal justice system requires that its workings be excluded from the ordinary rules of law and even logic that guarantee equal protection to racial minorities in our society.

And it is here, I suggest, that any self-respecting criminal justice professional is obliged to speak out against this Supreme Court's conception of the criminal justice system. We must reaffirm that there can be no justice in a system which treats people of color differently from white people, or treats crimes against people of color differently from crimes against white people.

We must reaffirm that racism is itself a crime, and that the toleration of racism cannot be justified by the supposed interest of society in fighting crime. We must pledge that when anyone—even a majority of the Supreme Court—tells us that a power to discriminate on grounds of race is necessary to protect society from crime, we will recognize that we are probably being sold another shipment of propaganda to justify repression. Let us therefore never fail to ask the question whether righteous rhetoric about protecting society from crime really refers to protecting only white people. And when the answer, as in the McCleskey case, is that protecting only white people is being described as "protecting society from crime," let us say that we are not so stupid as to buy this version of the Big Lie, nor so uncaring as to let it go unchallenged.

Eradicate Racism

Let us reaffirm that neither the toleration of racism by the Supreme Court nor the pervasiveness of racism in the criminal justice system can make it right, and that these things only make it worse. Let us reaffirm that racism exists, and is against the fundamental law of this Nation, whenever people of different races are treated differently by any public agency or institution as a consequence of their race and with no legitimate nonracial reason for the different treatment. Let us dedicate ourselves to eradicating racism, and declaring it unlawful, not simply in the superficial, short-lived situation where we can point to one or another specific decision-maker and show that his decisions were the product of conscious bigotry, but also in the far more basic, more intractable, and more destructive situation where hundreds upon hundreds of different public decision-makers, acting like Georgia's prosecutors and judges and juries—without collusion and in many cases without consciousness of their own racial biases—combine to produce a pattern that bespeaks the profound prejudice of an entire population.

147

"The only group which is disproportionately represented on death row is that of the white, non-minority male."

The Death Penalty Does Not Discriminate Against Blacks

Laurence W. Johnson

The death penalty is a just punishment that does not discriminate against blacks, Laurence W. Johnson argues in the following viewpoint. Johnson believes statistics show that white males, not blacks, are unfair victims of the death penalty. Blacks commit a higher percentage of murders, Johnson writes, and therefore a higher percentage of blacks should receive the death penalty. The author is a free-lance writer in Morton Grove, Illinois, and a contributor to the weekly newspaper *Human Events.*

As you read, consider the following questions:

1. What percentage of the murderers in 1987 were white, according to Johnson?
2. What conclusion does the author make after comparing the number of murderers in the U.S. with the number of prisoners on death row?
3. What does Johnson contend would happen if the U.S. executed killers of blacks as frequently as killers of whites?

Laurence W. Johnson, "Deceptive Tactics Mar Death Penalty Debate," *Human Events,* September 30, 1989. Reprinted with permission.

Opponents of capital punishment who claim that the system is racist (i.e., anti-minority) did not raise this claim when Ted Bundy, a white man convicted of murdering many whites, was executed. Yet, according to their primary thesis—that the system values white lives more than black lives by sentencing to death and executing murderers of white victims with greater zeal than murderers of black victims—the Bundy execution was a glaring example of what they call "victim-based racial discrimination."

Why did these critics refrain from denouncing the Bundy death sentence as an example of "white racism"? Very likely because they realized that even very casual observers would have immediately seen the absurdity of the argument.

Victim-Based Statistics

To say that "white racism" is at work when a white man is being sentenced to death is a macabre contrivance. The callous references to the white victims of murder in this "victim-based" concoction are appalling, especially when contrasted with the sympathetic references to the black lives which are allegedly devalued when killers of whites are sentenced to death.

The change over to the focus on statistics related to the race of the *victim* from the traditional one of race of the *offender* by the academic and minority group critics of the death penalty took place after it became clear that if any racial group was getting a disproportionate number of death sentences it was the white non-Hispanic group.

Figures relating to homicides are, necessarily, incomplete since not all killers are arrested and not all of those who are arrested are convicted. All of those who are sentenced to death and all of those who are executed are known, however.

The U.S. Bureau of Justice Statistics in the U.S. Department of Justice collects data from over 10,000 reporting law enforcement agencies. Among the many tables published in the annual "Sourcebook of Criminal Justice Statistics," perhaps the most useful for distinguishing between minority and non-minority (i.e., white) capital case defendants is the one which tabulates "Murders and non-negligent manslaughters known to police, by race, sex and ethnicity of victim and offender."

In the 1986 "Sourcebook," this Table (3.87) on page 266, lists 10,499 single-victim, single-offender homicides. Some 3,246 of these more than 10,000 murderers were white, non-Hispanic and 1,218 were white, Hispanic; 805 of those listed in the "white" category were of unknown ethnicity and 4,966 of the 10,499 killers were black. Thus it is clear that the black and Hispanic ("minority") murderers in this table far outnumber the white, non-Hispanic ones.

In the 1987 "Sourcebook," the same table (Table 3.111 on page

341) for the previous year lists 11,474 murders and non-negligent manslaughters. Of the murderers, 3,339 were white, non-Hispanic, 5,751 were black, 1,333 were white, Hispanic, and 768 were whites of unknown ethnicity. Again, we see that the white, non-minority killers constitute less than 40 per cent of the total.

Comparison to Death Sentence Records

Now we can compare the above data to the record of death sentences and executions in the U.S. that have taken place since the 1976 U.S. Supreme Court decision allowing states to constitutionally have death penalties that met the standards set by the court during the moratorium it imposed between 1968 and 1976.

LIES, DAMNED LIES AND STATISTICS

Mike Shelton. Reprinted with special permission of King Features Syndicate.

As of March 1, 1989, 2,134 prisoners were under sentence of death in the United States; 1,132 of these were white, 871 were black and 131 were Hispanic. From 1976 to March 1, 1986, 106 prisoners were executed by state authority; 59 of these were white and 47 were in the "minority" category (41 black and six Hispanic).

So while the evidence indicates that less than 40 per cent of homicides are committed by whites, more than half of the death sentences and more than half of the executions have been allocated to white prisoners.

All of this must be well known to those who claim the legal system demonstrates anti-minority racism and, because the evidence indicates the possibility of bias against white defendants, they avoid even mentioning it, let alone drawing inferences. Instead, they try to place all of the emphasis on their bizarre notion of victim-based discrimination.

Reading their papers on this theme, one may sometimes get the ghastly feeling that these critics are implying that the pathetic victims in death penalty cases are somehow responsible for discriminating.

Black Murderers, Black Victims

Another example of the hypocrisy of the victim-based critics is that, while they claim that sentencing to death murderers of whites more frequently than murderers of blacks constitutes "valuing white lives more than black lives," they refuse to discuss the fact that most murderers of blacks are themselves black. Thus, executing many killers of blacks would, inevitably, involve executing many black murderers.

If killers of blacks were executed more frequently than killers of whites, more black offenders would be executed than white offenders and, we can be absolutely sure, that would raise the claim of discrimination based upon the race of the offender.

In the 1987 ruling, in which the U.S. Supreme Court rejected the argument presented in the case *McCleskey v. Kemp*, that killers of white victims are discriminated against by too many death sentences, Justice William Brennan dissented, referring to society's treatment of the "minorities on Death Row." The facts show that the only group which is disproportionately represented on death row is that of the white, non-minority male.

"The imposition of capital punishment on a disproportionate number of lower class people . . . is a cruel irony. "

The Death Penalty Discriminates Against the Poor

Michael E. Endres

Michael E. Endres is a criminal justice professor at Xavier University in Cincinnati, Ohio. In the following viewpoint, excerpted from his book *The Morality of Capital Punishment*, Endres states that the poor are sentenced to death much more frequently than the wealthy. Inadequate legal representation and a bias against the poor often result in a death sentence for poor defendants, the author believes. The author maintains that only by abolishing the death penalty can social justice for the poor be achieved.

As you read, consider the following questions:

1. How does Endres describe the typical criminal defendant?
2. Why is the death penalty especially unjust for the poor, in the author's opinion?
3. How would society respond to the death penalty if the majority of defendants were middle-class instead of poor, according to Endres?

These excerpts are reprinted with permission from *The Morality of Capital Punishment: Equal Justice Under the Law?*, © 1985, by Michael E. Endres (paper, $5.95), published by Twenty-Third Publications, PO Box 180, Mystic, CT 06355.

Nowhere in American society are racial and socioeconomic divisions more apparent than in the criminal justice system. The typical criminal defendant is a lower class male, young, indigent, usually black. He is less educated than the general population, his employment history is less stable, and frequently he has problems with alcohol or drug abuse, mental illness or deficiency, etc. He is almost always represented by a public defender, or occasionally in rural areas, by a court-appointed attorney. The criminal court dockets in state jurisdictions contain few white-collar crime prosecutions. White-collar offenders are more often prosecuted in the federal district courts, when prosecuted at all. The same generalizations can be applied to members of organized crime, who are also underrepresented in the justice system clientele. The pronounced overrepresentation of lower class and minority people progresses through various levels of the justice system, from arrest through incarceration. It is generally recognized among criminologists that poor and minority persons are prone to arrest, conviction, and incarceration. . . .

Poverty and Death Row

Case studies on death row inmates indicate that whatever their racial origins, the condemned are invariably society's losers. They are poorer, less educated, if not less intelligent, less employable, and frequently they manifest abnormal emotional characteristics and alcohol and other substance abuse patterns. In short, as a collection, they closely resemble their brethren in the general population of the penal institution.

The bulk of criminal justice system clients are poor and black who are disproportionately represented in the system. Death row inmates are among the poorest. . . .

The injustice in inflicting the death penalty almost exclusively on the poor and minority people is compounded by the reality that these are precisely the groups from whom we ought to expect the least. It is they who have received the least of our economy's bounty. They have suffered benign neglect if not outright deprivation of their material needs. It is these segments of society that have suffered most from social injustice. They have resided in squalid, rat-infested slums, surrounded by criminal influences. They have benefitted least from the civilizing environments many of us take for granted. The imposition of capital punishment on a disproportionate number of lower class people, particularly minorities, is a cruel irony indeed. Are we incapable of recognizing the perpetuation of injustice in that?

There is no excuse for inhuman behavior; society has no choice but to protect itself against the violent offender. There are, however, different ways to do it and varying degrees of responsibility. It is an inept society that has plenty, yet permits a significant segment of its people to live in relative economic and cultural deprivation. Uncivilized behaviors are consistent with uncivilized conditions of life. It is also a cynical, selfish society that then permits the death penalty to be largely reserved for those who have derived the least benefit from society.

Reprinted with permission from *The California Prisoner.*

These are moral realities. They cannot be simply dismissed as effusions of a bleeding heart. Capital punishment is unjust. It magnifies the social injustice that characterizes the way of life of the most materially blessed society in all history. It also magnifies the routine deficiencies of the "justice" system. Poor people, many of whom bear the additional burden of minority identification, are less likely to elicit sympathy from officials in the justice system, jurors, or the community. (It is interesting to conjecture how long the death penalty would have lasted in America if the overwhelming percentage of the executed had been typically middle-class. Witness, e.g., our growing social and legal tolerance of marijuana possession and use as they spread into the middle classes.) Supreme Court decisions have sought to control arbitrariness by limiting discretion in the sentencing process. There is, however, little control over guilt determination processes or over the options of prosecutors in charging or plea bargaining.

Inevitability of Inequalities

It is a social and political reality that these deficiencies are not likely to disappear. Social "progress" is only a theory; it is not an accomplished fact. This side of the millenium, social class divisions will always persist. Differences in power will always exist. Inequalities before the law will always exist. They are predicated on our belief in the necessity and rightness of class divisions and on the self-interest which such divisions engender. Perfect justice is an ideal to be striven for. It is the most fundamental of all social values and virtues. It is worth all of the effort expended in its behalf. We cannot anticipate a perfectly just society, but can continue to make an effort. The abolition of capital punishment is a realistic, attainable milestone along the pathway to a just society.

"If guilty whites or wealthy people escape the gallows and guilty poor people do not, the poor or black do not become less guilty because the others escaped their deserved punishment."

Guilt Overrides the Importance of Death Penalty Discrimination

Ernest van den Haag

If a poor defendant is guilty, it does not matter that the death penalty discriminates against the poor, Ernest van den Haag states in the following viewpoint. Van den Haag argues that all murderers, whether rich or poor, deserve to be executed. The death penalty's only injustice is in society's failure to execute some wealthy murderers as well, he contends. The author, a well-known scholar and author on criminal justice issues, is a retired John M. Olin professor of jurisprudence and public policy at Fordham University in Bronx, New York.

As you read, consider the following questions:

1. What symbolic and moral importance does the death penalty have, in the author's opinion?
2. Why does van den Haag believe that poor people are convicted of murder more often than wealthy people?
3. What does the author believe about guilt and justice?

Ernest van den Haag, "Murderers Deserve the Death Penalty." This article appeared in the November 1989 issue and is reprinted with permission from *The World & I*, a publication of The Washington Times Corporation, copyright © 1989.

According to polls, more than 70 percent of Americans feel that murderers deserve the death penalty. Innocents should never be punished, but the punishment for people who have committed crimes should be reasonably proportionate to their culpability and to the seriousness of their crimes. Hence, if a burglar deserves imprisonment, a murderer deserves death—the only punishment appropriate to his crime. Murderers do not deserve to survive their victims.

Currently the law in the 37 states that have the death penalty provides that only those who have committed particularly heinous murders be sentenced to death. Usually, if a defendant is found guilty of murder, the jury, in a separate proceeding, is asked to determine whether the aggravating circumstances outweigh the mitigating ones (both listed in the law) and impose the death sentence only if that is the case. Thus, of the about 20,000 homicides committed annually in the United States, fewer than 300 lead to death sentences in any year. So far there have been fewer than 20 executions per year (after an average waiting time of six to seven years)—too few to reduce the number of death row inmates (about 2,100), which continues to climb.

Nonetheless, the death penalty retains great symbolic and moral importance. It indicates strongly that each of us has a right to only one life—his own—and that he risks losing it if he takes someone else's. . . .

The Advantages of Wealth

It is alleged that blacks and the poor often suffer the death penalty when equally guilty whites and wealthy people get away with murder. . . .

It is true that wealthy persons can afford a better legal defense than poor ones and thus may be able more readily to escape the death penalty. However, most murders are committed by poor persons, often during robberies. The wealthy rarely murder, just as they rarely commit burglaries, for obvious reasons. (They are more likely to commit "white-collar" crimes.)

No criminal justice system can totally avoid inequality despite all efforts to minimize it. Defendants are tried by different juries, judges, and lawyers—and even if they had the same amount of money to spend this would make a difference. All society can do is to make sure the defense attorneys are reasonably competent and that judges and juries are impartial. Even more important, of two persons guilty of murder, one may be found guilty and the other innocent if the first had the misfortune to have witnesses to the crime or other evidence against him and the second did not. Or one murderer may never be found, while the other is arrested immediately. We do not live in a perfect world. Equal punishment for equal guilt is an ideal to strive for, but we

157

should realize that it is not attainable. Systematic discrimination can be minimized—and great strides have been made in that direction—but accidental inequalities are hard to avoid. Unavoidably, some capriciousness and even some discrimination will remain in the system.

Maldistribution often is used to argue that the death penalty should be abolished. Never mind, this argument goes, that these objections would apply to the penal system as a whole. Death is different. What is tolerable for imprisonment is not tolerable for capital punishment. Perhaps. But I don't see how discrimination or capriciousness make a death sentence unjust if the defendant is guilty.

Guilt, Punishment, and Justice

Guilt is individual. If guilty whites or wealthy people escape the gallows and guilty poor people do not, the poor or black do not become less guilty because the others escaped their deserved punishment. Whether due to willful discrimination, capriciousness, or unavoidable accidental circumstances, some people will always get away with murder. Is that a reason to deny the justice of the punishment of those guilty persons who did not get away? Their guilt is not diminished by the escape of others, nor do they

158

deserve less punishment because others did not get the punishment they deserve. Justice involves punishment according to what is deserved by the crime and the guilt of the criminal—regardless of whether others guilty of the same crime escape.

Understanding Words in Context

Readers occasionally come across words they do not recognize. And frequently, because they do not know a word or words, they will not fully understand the passage being read. Obviously, the reader can look up an unfamiliar word in a dictionary. By carefully examining the word in the context in which it is used, however, the word's meaning can often be determined. A careful reader may find clues to the meaning of the word in surrounding words, ideas, and attitudes.

Below are excerpts from the viewpoints in this chapter. In each excerpt, one of the words is printed in italics. Try to determine the meaning of each word by reading the excerpt. Under each excerpt you will find four definitions for the italicized word. Choose the one that is closest to your understanding of the word.

Finally, use a dictionary to see how well you have understood the words in context. It will be helpful to discuss with others the clues that helped you decide on each word's meaning.

1. The innocent man's strong belief in justice was *VINDICATED* when the jury found him not guilty.

   VINDICATED means:

   a) proven correct   c) applied
   b) lost   d) reformed

2. No one has found evidence *REBUTTING* the conclusive studies of Baldus, who proved that the death penalty is racist.

   REBUTTING means:

   a) revealing   c) disproving
   b) rewriting   d) researching

3. Because the jury instructions were *EXPLICIT*, the jurors had no trouble understanding their duties.

EXPLICIT means:

a) precise   c) unclear
b) humorous   d) long

4. The civil rights workers dedicated themselves to *ERADICATING* racism.

ERADICATING means:

a) supporting   c) wiping out
b) explaining   d) denying

5. Racism in the criminal justice system remains an *INTRACTABLE* problem, in spite of the efforts of the civil rights movement.

INTRACTABLE means:

a) persistent   c) disruptive
b) minor   d) beneficial

6. Many death row inmates are alcohol and drug addicts who *MANIFEST* abnormal emotional characteristics.

MANIFEST means:

a) hide   c) control
b) lack   d) show

7. Prison inmates and their *BRETHREN* on death row share the common characteristics of poverty, substance abuse, lack of education, and unemployability.

BRETHREN means:

a) brothers   c) teachers
b) guards   d) lawyers

8. The poor are often ill because they reside in *SQUALID*, rat-infested slums where disease is present.

SQUALID means:

a) affordable   c) drafty
b) filthy   d) tiny

9. Many opponents believe the death penalty is *ARBITRARY* because no one can predict which murderers will be executed.

ARBITRARY means:

a) random   c) legal
b) just   d) immoral

Periodical Bibliography

The following articles have been selected to supplement the diverse views presented in this chapter.

American Civil Liberties Union	*The Death Penalty*. A briefing paper available from the American Civil Liberties Union, 132 West 43rd St., New York, NY 10036.
Frank Chapman	"The Death Penalty, U.S.A.: Racist and Class Violence," *Political Affairs*, July 1987.
Haven Bradford Gow	"Capital Punishment: The View from Middle America," *Lincoln Review*, Summer/Fall 1987.
Human Rights	"How Good Are Death Row Lawyers?" Spring 1989.
Irving Kristol	"Cries of 'Racism' Cow Crime Fighters," *The Wall Street Journal*, February 28, 1989.
Paul Marcotte	"Snoozing, Unprepared Lawyer Cited," *ABA Journal*, February 1991. Available from the American Bar Association, 750 N. Lake Shore Dr., Chicago, IL 60611.
Stanley Meisler	"Black Crime: Taking a Look Inward," *Los Angeles Times*, June 17, 1989.
John O'Sullivan	"Do the Right Thing—Suppress Crime," *National Review*, October 13, 1989.
Dee Reid	"Low IQ Is a Capital Crime," *The Progressive*, April 1988.
Ted Rohrlich	"Executions: Who Dies and Why," *Los Angeles Times*, April 2, 1990.
Social Justice	"Racism, Powerlessness, and Justice," entire issue on discrimination in the criminal justice system, Winter 1989. Available from University Microfilms, 300 N. Zeeb Rd., Ann Arbor, MI 48106.
William Wilbanks	"Statistics Show Racism a Myth," *Miami Review*, March 4, 1987. Available from Review Publications Inc., 100 Northeast 7th St., Miami, FL 33132.

Do Certain Crimes Deserve the Death Penalty?

Chapter Preface

In the past, Americans have used the death penalty as a punishment for a wide variety of crimes, from heresy to armed robbery. Today, however, execution is reserved almost exclusively for murderers. While many Americans are working to abolish even this use of the death penalty, others are proposing that it be expanded to apply to other crimes. These people assert that crimes such as drug dealing and terrorism pose as great a threat to society as murder and therefore warrant the death penalty.

For example, DeForest Z. Rathbone Jr., a member of a Massachusetts group dedicated to ending drug abuse, maintains that the death penalty is the best way to end the threat posed by America's growing drug problem. "The only feasible solution to the supply side of the drug-abuse equation is the death penalty for kingpin drug traffickers," Rathbone argues. While the U.S. Congress in 1988 did authorize the death penalty for drug-related killings, it is still considering whether to impose the death penalty on drug dealers. Experts who disagree with Rathbone hope Congress refrains from approving the death penalty for drug dealers. "Even hundreds of executions per year would leave the drug markets virtually unchanged," asserts Mark A. R. Kleiman, an author and professor at the John F. Kennedy School of Government at Harvard University in Cambridge, Massachusetts.

Similar debates exist regarding the appropriateness of the death penalty for terrorism, for the issues are the same: the effectiveness of the death penalty as a deterrent and the justness of execution as a punishment. The following chapter presents debates concerning the effectiveness and justness of the death penalty for drug dealers and terrorists.

*"It is time for [drug traffickers] to face the
punishment they deserve, and that punishment is
the death penalty."*

Drug Dealers Should Be Executed

Alfonse D'Amato and William F. Buckley Jr.

Recent polls show that many Americans view drug use as the nation's number one problem. In response to this public concern,
Republican Senator Alfonse D'Amato of New York has sponsored
the Senate version of the Drug Kingpin Death Penalty Act, which
would authorize the death penalty for drug dealers. In Part I of
the following viewpoint, D'Amato asserts that drug dealers are responsible for the drug deaths of thousands of Americans, and
therefore deserve the death penalty. In part II, William F. Buckley
Jr. argues that drug dealers should be sentenced to death because
their crimes deeply threaten American society. Buckley, a well-
known author and political commentator, is the editor-at-large for
the conservative magazine *National Review.*

As you read, consider the following questions:

1. What statistics does D'Amato cite to support his belief that
   drug dealers are a threat to American society?
2. Why does D'Amato hold drug dealers responsible for drug
   deaths?
3. Who should decide if drug dealers should be executed, in
   Buckley's opinion?

I

The deaths, disease, and misery caused by drugs are devastating to every community in this Nation, our inner cities, our small towns, and our suburban and rural areas. According to the 1990 survey conducted by the National Institute on Drug Abuse, among youth—12 to 17 years old—15.9 percent used an illicit drug in 1990 and 8.1 percent used an illicit drug at least once in December 1990. Department of Justice criminal statistics show that in 1989, 15,583 people were convicted for drug offenses in U.S. District Courts. The drug czar's office states that in 1989, there were a total of 1,075,728 drug arrests in Federal, State, and local jurisdictions, an increase of 26.5 percent from 1988 levels. The drug czar's office also estimates that there are 100,000 babies born each year harmed by the drug use of their mothers.

The Drug Kingpin Act

The Drug Kingpin Death Penalty Act provides for the death penalty for major drug dealers who distribute huge quantities of drugs; for example, over 66 pounds of heroin or 330 pounds of cocaine. It also applies to those who take in $10 million from drug trafficking in any 12-month period.

The second category of offenders eligible for capital punishment consists of drug kingpins who attempt to obstruct the investigation or prosecution of their activities by attempting to kill persons involved in the criminal justice process, or knowingly directing, advising, authorizing, or assisting another to attempt to kill such a person. The defendant would have to be a continuing criminal enterprise principal organizer, administrator, or leader, but would not necessarily have to traffic in the huge quantities that a "super kingpin" traffics in.

This aspect of the bill is a response to the flagrant and growing problem of extreme violence against witnesses in drug cases, as well as the increasing threat and reality of violence directed against criminal justice professionals.

The third category of death-eligible drug offenders fills a gap in existing law. The Anti-Drug Abuse Act of 1988 enacted provisions authorizing capital punishment for certain drug-related killings, but did not cover killings resulting from aggravated recklessness, or the death of users resulting from the knowing distribution of bad drugs.

The Drug Kingpin Death Penalty Act fills this gap by authorizing the death penalty where the defendant, intending to cause death or acting with reckless disregard for human life, engages in a Federal drug felony, and a person dies in the course of the offense or from the use of drugs involved in the offense.

This bill is virtually identical to death penalty language submitted by the drug czar. The only change I make in the drug czar's proposal is to make it clear that if those who commit these crimes are not sentenced to death, they will be sentenced to life in prison.

Conquering the Drug Problem

If all those caught producing or processing addictive drugs, plus all those caught selling addictive drugs in our country, were confronted with *capital punishment* administered without recourse, by local authorities throughout our 50 states—then gradually this intolerable situation would be ameliorated. And eventually conquered.

W. H. Long, *Manchester Union Leader*, October 3, 1989.

The drug traffickers know how dangerous their crimes are. They know that others will die as a result of their illegal activities. It is not one death, but tens of thousands of deaths, that result from their crimes. The drug traffickers are killing our kids. They are destroying our quality of life. It is time for them to face the punishment they deserve, and that punishment is the death penalty.

II

In New York state there is considerable frustration over the failure of the legislature to reimpose capital punishment. Gov. Mario Cuomo believes that the Supreme Court has a right to legalize killing unborn children but he does not appear to believe that the court has a right to legalize killing full-grown murderers. And frustration mounts.

Defining "Cruel and Unusual"

One hundred and thirteen people have been executed since the decision of the court in 1976 (Gregg vs. Georgia). It decreed the standards capital punishment legislation would need to meet if it wanted to escape death at the hands of the Eighth Amendment (which forbids cruel and unusual punishment).

Now the word "unusual" demands special examination. It would be "unusual" punishment to sentence a convicted man to be tossed into a cobra pit. It is also unusual to force a convicted man to expose his arm to a lethal injection—yet we are unaware of any legal arguments against the needle, especially when it is the execution mode of choice (some states do precisely that, grant the criminal his choice of two or more means of dying).

In order to be unusual in the sense of unconstitutional, the punishment needs to be archaic in the sense that it is thought to be cruelly archaic. And then in Coker vs. Georgia (1977) the court, with a heavy (7-2) majority, declared that punishment was "cruel" in the constitutionally prohibited sense if it imposed a penalty on a criminal disproportionate to the crime he had committed. In Coker, the court banned execution for rapists, the logic being that the victim in due course rises, and continues to live, whereas the rapist, if executed, will not rise again, at least not in this world.

All of which one gathers up and asks: Would it prove possible to institute death as the penalty for drug merchants? I would myself endorse such a penalty for drug merchants who sell the stuff to minors. Every now and then you could satisfy the standards of Coker vs. Georgia by pointing to a human corpse who had died of an overdose of the drugs. Would the court prohibit the execution of drug merchants who had pandered to minors?. . .

It is worth pondering: Should the Eighth Amendment deny to a government of the people by the people and for the people the right to decree the ultimate sentence as appropriate to a crime that deeply threatens that society? A few years ago there was no such thing as "crack" even as, a few years ago, there was no such things as AIDS. A call for capital punishment for drug merchants is consistent with the rhetorical gravity with which we refer to the menace of drugs. If drugs do indeed ruin and even kill, and it is illegal to sell such drugs, why is it inappropriate to punish Panderer A by execution, perhaps with the ripple effect of diverting Panderers B to Z to different professions?

Let the People Decide

Proponents of capital punishment have very nearly given up saying what is nevertheless true: Namely, that the extent to which such a penalty deters can only be known if it is comprehensively applied, and with some dispatch. We rue the Chinese students who are convicted on Monday and executed on Thursday. But we do indeed learn more about capital punishment as a deterrent than in America, where it takes 10 years to execute Ted Bundy. The Supreme Court should take a back seat. And my guess is that it would do so if the Cuomos of this world could be shunted aside, leaving it to the people, through their legislators, to judge when it is appropriate to take the life of the criminal.

"*Capital punishment for drug crimes represents . . . a backsliding in the moral evolution of our society.*"

Drug Dealers Should Not Be Executed

Sandra R. Acosta

In the following viewpoint, Sandra R. Acosta argues that sentencing drug dealers to death is an unjust punishment that will not deter drug crimes. While Acosta understands the anger and frustration Americans feel about the nation's drug problems, she asserts that executing drug dealers is not the solution. The author fears that once the nation accepts death sentences for drug dealers, it will find it easy to unjustly execute drug users, bankers who launder drug money, and others involved in drugs. Acosta, a Harvard University law student, is the president of the *Harvard Journal on Legislation*.

As you read, consider the following questions:

1. Why did the U.S. Supreme Court declare the death penalty unconstitutional in 1972, according to Acosta?
2. Why does the author believe that the death penalty will not deter drug dealing?
3. What does the author believe is the real cause of drug use and abuse?

Sandra R. Acosta, "Imposing the Death Penalty upon Drug Kingpins," *Harvard Journal on Legislation*, vol. 27, no. 579, 1990. Copied with permission granted by the *Harvard Journal on Legislation*, © 1990 by the President and Fellows of Harvard College.

There exists almost universal acceptance that the drug problem is "the worst disease that plagues our nation today," but no one is sure how to eradicate that disease. President George Bush unveiled his blueprint for a "War on Drugs" in September 1989, which resembled proposals by former President Ronald Reagan, calling for increased education, treatment, and enforcement of the drug laws. Congress is considering a much different measure: imposing the death penalty for certain drug-related crimes, some of which do not entail killing.

Passionate Debate

Capital punishment has been practiced in the United States since its founding, and always has excited passionate debate. That debate has led to certain reforms; for example, in 1972, the United States Supreme Court declared capital punishment unconstitutional as applied in two rape cases and one murder case then before it. The Court found that a Georgia statute which allowed untrammelled discretion of trial courts and juries in sentencing led to arbitrary and discriminatory sentencing practices, in violation of the eighth and fourteenth amendments. Georgia revised its statutory scheme to decrease the number of capital crimes and to provide greater guidance to juries in sentencing, and the Court in 1976 upheld a capital sentence imposed under the new guidelines.

Since then, nearly 200 executions have taken place nationwide, predominantly in Florida, Georgia, Texas, and Louisiana. Moreover, a 1986 poll indicated that approximately seventy percent of Americans favor the death penalty as punishment for murder. As the drug crisis ravages the country, many perceive that participation in the drug trade is "as horrendous as . . . first-degree murder." Several bills introduced in Congress respond to this sentiment by imposing the death penalty for serious drug trafficking crimes, despite the death penalty's traditional restriction to the most violent and aggravated crimes, usually murder.

Congress first authorized the death penalty for drug-related killings with the Anti-Drug Abuse Act of 1988. On November 21, 1989, Senator Alfonse "Gus" D'Amato (R-N.Y.), with thirty-four co-sponsors, introduced a bill entitled "Drug Kingpin Death Penalty Act." The bill, S. 1955, essentially provides the death penalty for the organizer of a "continuing criminal enterprise whose crime involves the manufacture or distribution of huge quantities of drugs," and who meets five criteria relating to the scope of the enterprise. Senator D'Amato believes this is the logical follow-up to prior law.

> [T]his bill sends a message. It says that if you are going to be involved in the business of death, in the sale and distribution of large quantities of cocaine, heroin, or other drugs, if you are

going to be involved in a criminal enterprise that takes in $10 million a year, understand what you are doing because you are killing, and you are participating in the death of innocents throughout the country—those who die of overdoses, and those who die because of the criminal activity of others.

Similarly, on May 18, 1989, Representative James A. Traficant (D-Ohio) introduced a bill amending section 848 of the Controlled Substances Act, to provide the death penalty for certain drug offenses. This bill provides that anyone who commits a drug violation involving ten or more kilograms of a preparation containing a detectable amount of heroin, cocaine, phenocyclidine, or a controlled substance analogue shall be sentenced to death or life imprisonment.

A Barbaric and Foolish Idea

The proposed drug death penalty is not only barbaric but also foolish: a temper tantrum masquerading as an act of government. It holds no promise for suppressing the drug trade, and may even be counterproductive.

Franklin E. Zimring, *The New York Times*, September 16, 1988.

As suggested above and discussed further below, the authorization of capital punishment for drug crimes represents a serious departure from prior legislative designations of crimes warranting this penalty and a backsliding in the moral evolution of our society. . . .

Crime and Punishment

Most general arguments in favor of and in opposition to capital punishment may be made with respect to the proposed drug legislation. The balance struck, however, should reflect the significant distinctions between the drug crimes contemplated by the new legislation and current capital crimes. Deterrence theory would argue that no rational person would risk his life to engage in a behavior that one could easily avoid or which provides no commensurate benefit. If we imposed the death penalty for jaywalking, certainly nobody would jaywalk. Yet, our society has purposely minimized the number of crimes which may be punished by death, reserving capital punishment for the most severely aberrant behaviors. This suggests that effectiveness yields to discomfort over the justice of imposing so harsh a penalty upon minor infractions.

In the drug context, deterrence is a particularly unconvincing rationale for the death penalty because drug trafficking is extremely lucrative and may be well worth the gamble, especially for the economically disenfranchised members of our society. Also, given how violent the internal drug scene is, the criminal justice system's penalties are unlikely to be a more effective deterrent than the violence to which one exposes himself upon entering the trade.

Because of the uncertain deterrence value of capital punishment, the debate usually shifts to retribution, which inherently contains the concept of proportionality. As discussed above, although imposing the death penalty on drug kingpins may pass constitutional muster, it would unquestionably stand at the outer limits of permissible punishment. Even if it is *permissible*, Congress has often recognized that it may not be *wise* to legislate to the Constitutional limits of its authority.

The "Slippery Slope"

In the first place, the extension of capital punishment to drug kingpins raises a "slippery slope" problem. Once Congress departs from the bright-line prerequisite of a victim's death in imposing capital punishment, it will be hard pressed to establish a new bright line. State legislatures might authorize the death sentence for lesser and lesser crimes, with the nexus between the "crime" and the abhorrent social effects becoming more and more attenuated. For example, President Bush's "Drug Czar" William Bennett proposed that "something analogous" to the death penalty be applied to "the high-level banker" who launders money for the drug trade. A just punishment?

Furthermore, many continue to question whether the United States should fight a war on drugs at all. They draw the now-familiar analogies to the Prohibition Era and propose the legalization of drugs, in the hope of eradicating at least the violence associated with the drug trade. However, this supply-side solution does nothing to curtail the remaining demand for drugs, which brings its own plethora of social ills. The legalization of alcohol did not remove the social ills accompanying the trade. Legalization shares this fatal flaw with the extension of capital punishment to drug kingpins: both measures attempt to eradicate the drug problem from the supply side. The real problems of drug use and abuse, of destruction of lives, arise on the demand side. Curtailing the importation of drugs and punishing the pushers cannot substitute for drug treatment, for the restoration of family values, or for the provision of employment; all of which may offer alternatives to the user's reliance upon drugs for both recreation and self-worth. [As Cahalan states,] "Thus it appears that the programs most likely to result in diminished drug use through all segments of the population would have to hold forth the promise of fairly immediate reinforcement of drug-free behavior through access to training and apprenticeships in decent jobs, as well as *realistic* avenues to better health and better family life."

The eighth amendment, as interpreted by the Supreme Court, must find its meaning in the evolving standards of decency of a maturing society. Many, if not most, Americans may favor the death penalty for drug kingpins, believing it to be the only effective solution to a drug crisis which might destroy our society. The flaws in this causal analysis have been ignored or adopted by legislators who encourage the false hopes of their constituents by proposing supply-side solutions to a demand-side problem. The courts should not mistake this reactionary behavior for the reflective and progressive restrictions on the use of capital punishment which have characterized our criminal justice system for centuries, and which provide the true standards by which the constitutionality of the proposed legislation should be measured.

"A public execution . . . will serve notice on all potential terrorist killers that the world community will not give way to their despicable acts."

Terrorists Should Be Executed

Robert A. Friedlander

In recent decades, nations all over the world have struggled to determine how best to fight terrorism. In the following viewpoint, Robert A. Friedlander asserts that terrorism is so heinous a crime that it must be punished by death. Friedlander believes executions will protect society by deterring other terrorists. Friedlander is a law professor at Ohio Northern University's Pettit College of Law in Ada. He is also the chairman of the International Law Association's Committee on International Terrorism.

As you read, consider the following questions:

1. Why does Friedlander believe public executions will have a strong effect on Middle Eastern terrorists?
2. Why does the author argue that the death penalty is simply a form of self-defense?
3. Why does Friedlander support the abduction of terrorists?

Robert A. Friedlander, "Punishing Terrorists: A Modest Proposal," *Ohio Northern University Law Review*, vol. 13, no. 1, 1986. Reprinted wth permission.

If we do what should be done, we as a nation, with the cooperation of the free world (if such cooperation is given), can control terrorism, though we will never be able to eliminate it altogether. But control is a matter of degree, and it must be conceded that we are far from reaching a satisfactory level on the preventive scale. . . .

Thus, I would like to make a modest proposal, borrowing the terminology of Jonathan Swift, but applying, in the manner of my ancestors, Old Testament justice. In short, what I am recommending is not only the death penalty for terrorists who cause loss of life in any fashion, but also for the court's capital sentence to be carried out via public execution. Humiliate the terrorists. Shame them. Degrade them. Treat them as the monsters that they really are.

Swift and certain justice, implemented by any apprehending or receiving state, for seized or extradited terrorists, may not always, or often, deter. But it will *always* put future terrorists on notice that the hangman's noose, the electric chair, the gas chamber, or the firing squad will be their inevitable fate, if any are taken alive after their heinous crimes. More significantly, especially for Middle Eastern terrorist offenders, the recognition of the loss of face, personal humiliation, and physical degradation that goes with a public execution may have some effect upon the terrorists' not altogether irrational minds.

A public execution, televised if possible, will serve notice on all potential terrorist killers that the world community will not give way to their despicable acts. Like Mrs. Marilyn Klinghoffer, civilized humanity will metaphorically spit in their bestial faces prior to inflicting upon them the same denial of life that they have inflicted upon others. They will have died in the kind of shame commensurate with their monstrous crimes.

Moral Justification

Admittedly, the death penalty is perhaps the most controversial issue in the administration of American criminal justice, although the exclusionary rule is not far behind. The primary touchstone of the debate for both proponents and opponents appears to be the role of deterrence. As yet, no one has produced a decisive study one way or the other that the death penalty either deters or fails to deter potential murderers. A quantitative analysis with a demonstrable, verifiable conclusion has yet to be produced.

On the other hand, the Anglo-American legal system is based upon the belief in the worth, the sanctity, and the importance of one human life. If the death penalty deters merely one would-be terrorist murderer (let alone more than one), and saves but one innocent victim, then it is morally justified. Critics of the

175

death penalty erroneously focus on sheer numbers on death row rather than upon the more relevant issue of the preservation of human life. The key here, as with terrorism in general, is the innocence of the victim, who is worth saving, as opposed to the malicious and premeditated or criminally reckless act of a first-degree terrorist murderer, who is definitely not worth saving.

Reprinted with special permission of © 1986 North American Syndicate, Inc.

As far back as the eighteenth century, the influential German moral philosopher, Immanuel Kant, urged the necessity of capital punishment for the purpose of societal retribution. The doctrine of retribution is not only Biblical in origin, but it also has underlain the criminal laws of all civilized societies and governments. Retribution is one of the four basic principles of the criminal sanction, and its function is to compensate society on an emotional and psychological level, as well as from a cost-benefit-analysis perspective. Retribution represents a moral judgment of society or an expression of moral feeling toward the wrongdoer. According to some criminologists, "murder is so heinous a crime that only the most extreme punishment we possess can uphold the moral code."

Society's Self-Defense

The doctrine of justifiable self-defense has been for centuries an engrained part of Anglo-American law. Utilizing deadly force is permissible by an innocent victim, who is actually threatened by deadly force. As one criminal scholar observes: "[I]f killing in self-defense is accepted as justifiable, it is accepted as modifying the prohibitory norm against killing; killing in self-defense is not wrong, the actor is accountable for it, and so far from blaming him we say that he was quite right to act as he did.". . .

Abducting Terrorists

Apprehension of terrorist offenders, responsible for capital crimes, is difficult, if not impossible, to achieve in the present world political climate. This is evidenced by the failure of the Lebanese Government to arrest and deliver the TWA Flight 847 killers of Navy Diver Robert Dean Stethem and the refusal of both Italy and Yugoslavia to arrest the *Achille Lauro* master plotter, Mohammed Abul Abbas. Extradition may be the theoretical way around terrorist impasse, but often it does not work. Therefore, one is left with the only remaining viable option— which is good law and good policy—abducting terrorist offenders. In the words of one knowledgeable contributor to this symposium, "the U.S. should exercise its legal right to engage in self-help."

Of course, as a *New York Times* editorial points out, abducting terrorists for purposes of trial "[is] no substitute for joint action when it can be negotiated. But [it] can bring some murderers to justice. . . ." Grabbing a few terrorists, trying them in American courts, subjecting those convicted to capital punishment for their despicable crimes, and carrying out that sentence via public execution, without an inordinate delay, may do wonders for restoring public order to a global community on the brink of terrorist chaos.

Capital punishment is desirable; it is necessary; and it represents a moral as well as a legal judgment. Free societies which have abolished it have not seen a corresponding decrease in their murder rates. Indeed, the elimination of capital punishment in Western Europe, England, and Israel has favored the terrorist and his reprehensible acts. Heinous crimes deserve the ultimate punishment. Otherwise society betrays itself.

There are times when humankind cries out for vengeance. Those awful cries must be heard, for terrorism, in the Biblical phrase, is truly the calamity of the innocent. A noted legal philosopher plaintively asks: "Can we assure the members of organized [terrorist] crime rings and bands of assassins that no matter what suffering they inflict upon their neighbors, the worst they can expect to suffer—if they are caught, tried, and convicted—is a life sentence which they know is seldom served?"

Let us begin at long last to terrorize the terrorist barbarians. Only then will the light of civilization begin to point the way out of the dark tunnel of global terror-violence.

"Never in history has the threat of execution halted terrorism or political crime."

Terrorists Should Not Be Executed

Amnesty International

Amnesty International is a worldwide human rights group that works for the release of nonviolent political prisoners. Amnesty supports the total abolition of the death penalty throughout the world. In the following viewpoint, excerpted from *When the State Kills* . . . , the authors argue that the death penalty will not deter terrorists and is not a just punishment for political crimes. In addition, the authors maintain that most terrorists are accustomed to risking their lives for a cause, and some might even view execution as an incentive.

As you read, consider the following questions:

1. Death penalty supporters argue that executions fulfill an important need for society. What do the authors cite as the two major flaws of this argument?
2. Why does Amnesty International believe it is dangerous to execute terrorists for political crimes?
3. Rather than protecting society, what does the death penalty do, in the authors' opinion?

The case for the death penalty rests on a claim that executions fulfill important needs of society that cannot be met in other ways. Whether executions are carried out in public or shielded from view behind prison walls, the argument used is that the death penalty is necessary, at least temporarily, for the good of society.

The argument has two major flaws.

First, it can never justify the violation of fundamental human rights. Torture cannot be justified by arguing that in some situations it might be useful. International law clearly states that a cruel, inhuman or degrading punishment is always prohibited, even in time of the gravest public emergency.

Second, despite centuries of experience with the death penalty and many scientific studies of the relationship between that penalty and crime rates, there is no convincing evidence that it is uniquely able to protect society from crime or to meet the demands of justice. In many ways it does the opposite. . . .

The Death Penalty and Political Violence

Bombings, kidnappings, assassinations of public officials, aircraft hijackings and other politically motivated acts of violence often kill or maim not only the intended targets of attack but bystanders as well. These acts understandably provoke strong public outcry and may result in demands for the death penalty to be used. Yet as public officials responsible for fighting such crimes have repeatedly pointed out, executions are as likely to increase acts of terror as to stop them.

As a professor of criminology in Canada has observed: "Those who really think that the reinstitution of capital punishment will put an end to, or will produce a reduction in, the number of terrorist incidents are either extremely naive or under an illusion. Standard punishments, including the death penalty, do not impress terrorists or other political criminals who are ideologically motivated and dedicated to make sacrifices for the sake of their cause. . . . Moreover, terrorist activities are fraught with danger and the terrorist runs all kinds of deadly risks without being intimidated by the prospect of immediate death. Is it conceivable that he will be deterred by the remote and low risk of the death penalty?"

Those responsible for drafting laws have pointed out how hard it is to define acts of terror in legal statutes. It is difficult, if not impossible, to isolate politically motivated crimes warranting the death penalty without, in effect, punishing the perpetrators for their political views as well as for their crimes. Furthermore, such isolation may well confer special recognition on the deeds of violent groups—something governments usually seek to avoid.

179

Executions for politically motivated crimes may result in greater publicity for acts of terror, thus drawing increased public attention to the perpetrators' political agenda. Such executions may also create martyrs whose memory becomes a rallying point for their organizations. For some men and women convinced of the legitimacy of their acts, the prospect of suffering the death penalty may even serve as an incentive. Far from stopping violence, executions have been used as the justification for more violence as opposition groups have seized the opportunity to bolster their legitimacy by using in reprisal the same "death penalty" that governments claim the right to impose.

A Futile Effort

The most important insight about terrorism is that it is community-based—an outgrowth of the social dynamics of particular communities where individuals feel themselves to be beleaguered and ignored both at home and by the international community. When they feel themselves under siege, community members begin to tolerate more extreme behavior in the name of community causes. The surest sign of imminent terrorist activity is unwillingness of community leaders to condemn their own extreme elements for fear of losing overall support. . . .

Because community members see their causes as righteous, indeed even sacred, the terrorist acts in their name are often perceived as virtuous. And because these acts are based in the community, attacking individual terrorists is a futile control device. Individuals who are arrested or executed become martyrs to the community cause and are quickly replaced by others inspired by their terrorism.

William O. Beeman, *Los Angeles Times*, January 9, 1986.

British authorities ruling Palestine hanged several members of the underground Zionist Irgun organization in the 1940s following their conviction on charges of bombings and other violent attacks. Menachem Begin, former Irgun leader and later Prime Minister of Israel, reportedly told a former British Government minister that the executions had "galvanized" his group, which subsequently hanged several British soldiers in retaliation. Menachem Begin said the hangings "got us the recruits that we wanted, and made us more efficient and dedicated to the cause . . . you were not sentencing our terrorists to death, you were sentencing a lot of your own people, and we decided how many."

On 17 September 1975 a firing squad in Spain executed five members of opposition groups who had been convicted after summary trials of killing members of the government's security forces. Four days later three police officers were shot dead and a fourth fatally wounded, reportedly in reprisal.

In August 1980 the Government of Angola convicted nine members of the opposition group *União Nacional para a Independência Total de Angola* (UNITA), National Union for the Total Independence of Angola, on charges of organizing a bombing campaign. The nine prisoners were executed on 22 August, the day after sentencing. On 23 August UNITA "sentenced" to death 15 people described as government soldiers and immediately executed them.

As France's then Minister of Justice, Robert Badinter, said in 1985: ". . . history and contemporary world events refute the simplistic notion that the death penalty can deter terrorists. Never in history has the threat of execution halted terrorism or political crime. Indeed, if there is one kind of man or woman who is not deterred by the threat of the death penalty, it is the terrorist, who frequently risks his life in action. Death has an ambiguous fascination for the terrorist, be it the death of others by one's own hand, or the risk of death for oneself. Regardless of his proclaimed ideology, his rallying cry is the fascist *'viva la muerte'* [Long live death]."...

A Pseudo-Solution

The death penalty does not stamp out crime. It is a pseudo-solution which diverts attention from the measures needed to prevent crime, by creating the false impression that decisive measures are being taken. The death penalty does not protect society, but rather distracts attention from the urgent need for methods of effective protection which at the same time uphold and enhance respect for human rights and life.

Like torture, the death penalty is cruel, inhuman and degrading. It destroys human lives and violates human rights. The alternative to the death penalty, like the alternative to torture, is abolition.

Distinguishing Bias from Reason

When dealing with controversial subjects, many people allow their feelings to dominate their powers of reason. Thus, one of the most important critical thinking skills is the ability to distinguish between statements based upon emotion or bias and conclusions based upon a rational consideration of the facts. For example, consider the following statement: "Terrorists should die in the kind of shame commensurate with their monstrous crimes." This statement is biased. The author is using emotional, exaggerated language rather than reason to express his opinion. In contrast, the statement, "Because terrorists threaten the public's safety, all governments must be aware of the goals and methods of terrorist groups" is a reasonable statement. Governments are responsible for the safety of their citizens. The author is using this fact to substantiate his opinion that governments should increase their knowledge of terrorist groups.

The following statements are adapted from opinions expressed in the viewpoints in this chapter. Consider each statement carefully. *Mark R for any statement you believe is based on reason or a rational consideration of the facts. Mark B for any statement you believe is based on bias, prejudice, or emotion. Mark I for any statement you think is impossible to judge.*

If you are doing this activity as a member of a class or group, compare your answers with those of others. Be able to defend your answers. You may discover that others come to different conclusions than you do. Listening to the rationale others present for their answers may give you valuable insights in distinguishing between bias and reason.

> R = *a statement based upon reason*
> B = *a statement based upon bias*
> I = *a statement impossible to judge*

1. Many murderers state that they do not consider the possibility of punishment when committing their crimes. This makes it unlikely that the death penalty would deter these criminals.

2. While curtailing the importation of drugs and punishing drug dealers may decrease the supply of drugs, it will not help addicts beat their dependency on drugs.

3. The death penalty for drugs is a barbaric, foolish idea.

4. Cries for vengeance must be heard, for terrorism is truly the calamity of the innocent.

5. The death penalty destroys human lives and violates human rights.

6. Nearly all other western industrialized nations have abolished the death penalty. To reflect the values of western society, the United States should also abolish the death penalty.

7. America's drug problem is the worst disease that has ever plagued a nation.

8. Criminals condemned to be executed often receive much publicity. This publicity might actually entice some criminals to commit crimes.

9. Since most people fear death above all else, it can be assumed that the death penalty will deter some criminals.

10. Like torture, the death penalty is cruel, inhuman, and degrading.

11. Terrorists frequently risk their lives to achieve their goals. It is unlikely, therefore, that the threat of the death penalty will deter terrorists.

12. Those who support the death penalty for drug dealers have no concern for justice and civil rights.

13. Those who really think that the reinstitution of capital punishment will put an end to terrorist incidents are either extremely naive or under an illusion.

14. If the death penalty deters merely one would-be terrorist murderer and saves but one innocent victim, then it is morally justified.

15. Prisoners on death row wait an average of eight years to be executed. The process of death penalty sentencing must be reformed to reduce this waiting period.

Organizations to Contact

The editors have compiled the following list of organizations that are concerned with the issues debated in this book. All of them have publications or information available for interested readers. The descriptions are derived from materials provided by the organizations. This list was compiled upon the date of publication. Names and phone numbers of organizations are subject to change.

American Bar Association (ABA)
750 N. Lake Shore Dr.
Chicago, IL 60611
(312) 988-5000

The ABA, the foremost legal organization in the U.S., works to improve the civil and criminal justice systems. The organization opposes the death penalty for mentally retarded murderers and those under eighteen. The ABA conducts research and educational programs, and publishes the *ABA Newsletter* and the monthly *ABA Journal*.

American Civil Liberties Union (ACLU) Capital Punishment Project
122 Maryland Ave. NE
Washington, DC 20002
(202) 234-4890

Founded in 1920, the ACLU champions the rights set forth in the Declaration of Independence and the Constitution. The Union is one of America's oldest civil liberties organizations. Staunch opponents of the death penalty, members of the Union defend death row inmates and attempt to postpone executions. The ACLU publishes the quarterly newspaper *Civil Liberties* and various pamphlets, books, and position papers.

American Correctional Association (ACA)
8025 Laurel Lakes Ct.
Laurel, MD 20707
(301) 206-5100

The ACA is an organization of corrections professionals, including prison wardens and parole officers. It works to improve prison and correctional standards by providing information on the practical aspects of criminal justice, including the effectiveness of punishments such as the death penalty. The Association publishes books and the monthly periodical *Corrections Today*.

Americans for Effective Law Enforcement (AELE)
5519 N. Cumberland Ave., #1008
Chicago, IL 60656-1471
(312) 763-2800

AELE attempts to help prosecutors, police, and the courts promote fairer, more effective administration of criminal law and equal justice, including unbiased sentences for all criminals. Some of the organization's many monthly publications include *Jail and Prisoner Law Bulletin* and *Security Legal Update*.

Amnesty International USA
322 Eighth Ave.
New York, NY 10001
(212) 807-8400

Amnesty International is an international human rights organization that opposes the death penalty. Among Amnesty's many publications on the death penalty are the pamphlet *The Death Penalty: Cruel & Unusual Punishment* and the book *A Punishment in Search of a Crime*. The organization also publishes the bimonthly newsletter *Amnesty Action*.

The Heritage Foundation
214 Massachusetts Ave. NE
Washington, DC 20002
(202) 546-4400

The Foundation is a public policy research institute that supports the death penalty to reduce and deter crime. Heritage Foundation publications include the pamphlet *A Note on the Sentencing of Criminals*, the quarterly journal *Policy Review*, and the periodic *Backgrounder* and *Heritage Lectures*.

The Lincoln Institute for Research and Education
1001 Connecticut Ave. NW, Suite 1135
Washington, DC 20036
(202) 223-5112

The Lincoln Institute studies public policy issues affecting black Americans. The Institute, which supports the death penalty, sponsors conferences and publishes the *Lincoln Review*, a monthly journal of political and social opinion.

NAACP Legal Defense and Educational Fund
99 Hudson St., Suite 1600
New York, NY 10013
(212) 219-1900

The NAACP Legal Defense and Educational Fund is the legal branch of the National Assocation for the Advancement of Colored People. The Fund opposes the death penalty and works to end discrimination in the criminal justice system. In addition to compiling statistics on the death penalty, the Fund publishes legal materials, brochures, reports, and the quarterly *Equal Justice*.

National Center for Juvenile Justice
701 Forbes Ave.
Pittsburgh, PA 15219
(412) 227-6950

The National Center for Juvenile Justice compiles statistics on juvenile crime and punishment. The Center does not take a stance on the death penalty for juveniles, but provides information on the issue. It maintains research files and a library of one thousand volumes on juvenile justice and operates a resource center. In addition to monographs, reports, and studies, the Center publishes the annuals *Today's Delinquent* and *Juvenile Court Statistics*.

185

National Coalition to Abolish the Death Penalty
1325 G St. NW, Lower Level B
Washington, DC 20005
(202) 347-2411

The National Coalition to Abolish the Death Penalty is a collection of more than 115 groups working together to stop executions in the U.S. The organization compiles statistics on the death penalty. To further its goal, the Coalition publishes *Legislative Action to Abolish the Death Penalty*, information packets, pamphlets, and research materials.

The Sentencing Project
918 F St. NW, Suite 501
Washington, DC 20005
(202) 628-0871

The Sentencing Project supports establishing and improving punishment alternatives to imprisonment and the death penalty. To promote its belief in alternative sentencing, the Project sponsors seminars and speakers and publishes the annual *National Directory of Felony Sentencing Services*.

U.S. Department of Justice
Constitution Avenue and Tenth Street
Washington, DC 20530
(202) 514-2000

The Department of Justice compiles statistics on crime and the criminal justice system. Write for information and a list of publications.

Victims of Crime and Leniency (VOCAL)
PO Box 1283
114 N. Hull St.
Montgomery, AL 36103
(205) 262-7197

VOCAL, an organization of victims of crime, seeks to ensure that victims' rights are recognized and protected. It supports the death penalty and measures to reduce crime and increase punishment for criminals. VOCAL publications include the quarterly *VOCAL Voice* and a newsletter.

Washington Legal Foundation
1705 N St. NW
Washington, DC 20036
(202) 857-0240

The Foundation is a legal research organization that represents crime victims seeking restitution. It supports the death penalty as a just punishment for murder. The Foundation publishes the monograph *Capital Punishment* as well as the weekly *Legal Backgrounders* and the monthly *WLF Working Papers Studies*.

Bibliography of Books

Amnesty International — *United States of America: The Death Penalty.* London: Amnesty International Publications, 1987.

Johanness Andenaes — *Punishment and Deterrence.* Ann Arbor: University of Michigan Press, 1974.

Robert M. Baird and Stuart A. Rosenbaum — *Philosophy of Punishment.* Buffalo: Prometheus Books, 1988.

Hugo Adam Bedau — *Death Is Different: Studies in the Morality, Law, and Politics of Capital Punishment.* Boston: Northeastern University Press, 1987.

Walter Berns — *For Capital Punishment: Crime and the Morality of the Death Penalty.* New York: Basic Books, 1974.

William J. Bowers — *Legal Homicide: Death as Punishment in America, 1864-1982.* Boston: Northeastern University Press, 1984.

Shirley Dicks — *Death Row: Interviews with Inmates, Their Families, and Opponents of Capital Punishment.* Jefferson, NC: McFarland & Co., 1990.

Donald D. Hook and Lothar Kahn — *Death in the Balance: The Debate over Capital Punishment.* Lexington, MA: Lexington Books, 1989.

Joseph B. Ingle — *Last Rights: Thirteen Fatal Encounters with the State's Justice.* Nashville: Abingdon Press, 1990.

David Lester — *The Death Penalty: Issues and Answers.* Springfield, IL: Charles C. Thomas, 1987.

Massachusetts General Court Senate and House of Representatives Committees on Capital Punishment — *Capital Punishment: Nineteenth-Century Arguments.* New York: Arno Press, 1974.

Louis P. Masur — *Rites of Execution: Capital Punishment and the Transformation of American Culture.* NY: Oxford University Press, 1989.

Stephen Nathanson — *An Eye for an Eye? The Morality of Punishing by Death.* Totowa, NJ: Rowman & Littlefield, 1987.

Michael L. Radelet, ed. — *Facing the Death Penalty: Essays on a Cruel and Unusual Punishment.* Philadelphia: Temple University Press, 1989.

Tom Sorell — *Moral Theory and Capital Punishment.* Oxford: Basil Blackwell in association with Open University, 1987.

Victor L. Streib — *Death Penalty for Juveniles.* Bloomington, IN: Indiana University Press, 1987.

Ernest van den Haag — *Punishing Criminals: Concerning a Very Old and Painful Question.* New York: Basic Books, 1975.

Ernest van den Haag and John P. Conrad — *The Death Penalty: A Debate.* New York: Plenum Press, 1983.

Welsh S. White — *The Death Penalty in the Eighties: An Examination of the Modern System of Capital Punishment.* Ann Arbor: University of Michigan Press, 1987.

William Wilbanks — *The Myth of a Racist Criminal Justice System.* Monterey, CA: Brooks/Cole Publishing Company, 1987.

Index

Abbas, Mohammed Abu, 177
Acosta, Sandra R., 169
Ad Hoc Committee on Federal Habeas Corpus in Capital Cases (Powell Committee), 130-131, 134, 135-136
America, 111
American Bar Association, 134, 136
Amnesty International, 178
Amsterdam, Anthony G., 142
Anti-Drug Abuse Act (1988), 166, 170
assassination, 32

Badinter, Robert, 181
Baldus, David, 123-124, 144, 145-146
Barfield, Velma, 104
Beccaria, Cesare, 21
Beeman, William O., 180
Begin, Menachem W., 180
Bellotti v. Baird (1979), 87-88
Bennett, William, 172
Bentham, Jeremy, 25
Bible, 69, 175, 176, 177
Bieler, Glenn M., 86
Bishop, Arthur Gary, 99
blacks
  death penalty discriminates against, 78-79, 106-108, 142-147, 153
  con, 72, 85, 103, 148-151, 157
Bosket, Willie, 71
Brennan, William J., Jr., 151
Briley, James and Linwood, 102-103
Buckley, William F., Jr., 165
Bundy, Theodore, 64, 65, 71, 149, 168
Buono, Angelo, 60
Bush, George, 170

Calder, R.L., 45
California, 134
  executions in, 58, 110
Canada, homicides in, 50, 112
Chapman, Frank, 146
Chicano, Mark, 68
China, capital punishment in, 63, 168
Christianity, 18, 49, 77-78
  supports capital punishment, 67-73
  con, 74-81

cities, 50
civil rights
  death sentence appeals protect, 133-136
  con, 127-132
clemency, executive, 51
Cohen, Bernard, 98
Coker v. Georgia (1977), 168
Cole, James, 123-124
Controlled Substances Act Amendment (1989), 171
crime
  capital offenses, 48, 52
  causes of, 49, 51, 52
  death penalty discourages, 17-20, 30, 46
  con, 21-26, 48-49, 51, 78, 111, 124, 125, 147
  recidivism, 103
Crowe, Robert E., 41
Cuomo, Mario M., 100, 109, 167, 168
Curtis, George, 76

D'Amato, Alfonse, 165, 170
Darden, Willie Jasper, 100-101, 107-108
Darrow, Clarence, 47
Dear, John, 74
death penalty
  benefits of
    deters crime, 17-20, 42, 46, 72
    con, 21-26, 48-49, 58, 78, 111, 171-172, 179, 181
    deters murder, 28-29, 30-31, 84-85, 98, 113-118
    con, 36, 37, 90, 111-112, 119-126
    is effective, 97-104
    con, 105-112
    is just, 57-60
    con, 61-66
    is moral, 32-33, 59, 72, 175
    con, 37, 40, 58, 62
  Christianity supports, 67-73
    con, 74-81
  costs of, 100, 110-111
  discriminates
    against blacks, 78-79, 106-108, 142-147
    con, 72, 85, 103, 148-151

against the poor, 78, 152-155
  con, 156-159
drug dealers deserve, 165-168
  con, 169-173
for juvenile murderers, 82-85
  con, 86-90
purposes of
  as retribution, 27-34, 59, 60, 71-72,
    90, 104, 117-118, 172, 176
    con, 23, 25-26, 35-40, 42, 48, 59,
      62, 106, 112
  for protection, 41-46, 71
    con, 47-52, 79
  for revenge, 36-37, 42, 44, 48, 59,
    106, 112
sentence appeals undermine,
  127-132
  con, 133-136
terrorists deserve, 174-177
  con, 178-181
death row
  conditions, 75
  escapes from, 102-103
  number of inmates on, 63, 76, 131,
    150, 157, 175-176
  number of minorities on, 106, 146,
    150, 151, 153
Denning, Lord Alfred, 104
Dred Scott v. Sandford (1857), 143
drug dealers
  should be executed, 165-168
    con, 169-173
Drug Kingpin Death Penalty Act,
  166-167, 170-171

Eddings v. Oklahoma (1979), 88
Ehrlich, Isaac, 114, 115, 123-124
Endres, Michael E., 152
executions
  brutalize society, 25-26, 36, 40,
    80-81
    con, 31, 32-33, 59
  constitutional moratorium on, 62,
    167, 170
  costs of, 100, 111
  deter crime, 99-100, 114
    con, 40, 112, 124, 180-181
  number performed, 76, 157, 167,
    170
  of minorities, 106-107, 146, 150
  of rapists, 168
  of the innocent
    are unacceptable, 38, 65-66,
      134-135
      con, 33-34, 43, 59-60, 73, 116

of women, 103-104
public, 175

Florida
  death sentencing in, 108
  executions in, 64, 100, 111, 170
Friedlander, Robert A., 174
Furman v. Georgia (1972), 110

Garey, Margaret, 110
Georgia
  capital punishment law, 72, 146,
    170
    racial discrimination in, 78-79,
      143, 144, 145, 146, 147, 170
  executions in, 75-76, 146, 170
  homicides in, 144
  Supreme Court, 101
Gillespie, L. Kay, 104
Gilmore, Gary Mark, 98-99
Goldberg, Steven, 113
Great Britain
  capital punishment in, 19, 44, 48,
    52, 116, 177
Greeley, Horace, 35
Gregg v. Georgia (1976), 98, 167

habeas corpus
  appeals should be limited, 128-129,
    130, 131-132
    con, 134-135, 136
Hahn, Reuben, 73
Hand, Samuel, 29, 31
Harris, Robert Alton, 58, 59, 60
Healey, John G., 125
Hearst, William Randolph, 49
Henry, Carl F.H., 69
Hispanics, 149, 150
homicide. See murder

Illinois, 111-112
imprisonment, 58, 143-144, 158
  costs of, 100, 110-111
  deters crime, 48, 120-121, 122, 123,
    125
    con, 71, 84-85, 102-103, 117
  punishes effectively, 36, 38
    con, 29, 34, 42, 43, 68
Ingle, Joseph B., 80

Jesus, 69, 73, 75, 78, 79, 90, 91
Johnson, Laurence W., 148
Jones, Jenkin Lloyd, 98
Kant, Immanuel, 68, 176

Kelly, Frank V., 101
King, Rev. Martin Luther, Jr., 79
Klinghoffer, Marilyn, 175

lawyers, 42-43, 109-110, 136
Lebanon, 177
Lee, Robert W., 97
Long, W.H., 167

McCleskey v. Kemp (1987), 143-144, 147
McCleskey, Warren, 143, 144, 145, 146
Massachusetts, 37
Miami Herald, 65, 100, 111
Michigan, 111-112
Mill, John Stuart, 27
Moore, John, 19
Moore, William Neal, 76-78, 79, 81, 101-102
murder, 157
  death penalty deters, 19, 42, 44, 72, 98-99, 113-118
    con, 26, 49-50, 106-107, 111-112, 119-126
  justifies the death penalty, 68, 69, 70, 73, 176
    con, 65, 80, 81
    for juveniles, 82-85
      con, 86-90
    to protect society, 27-34, 43, 45-46, 58-59, 72-73, 177
      con, 35-40, 51, 79

NAACP Legal Defense Fund, 143
Nathanson, Stephen, 119
National Coalition to Abolish the Death Penalty, 78
National Council of Churches Defense Fund, 108
National Institute on Drug Abuse, 166
National Organization for Women, 104
New York
  capital punishment in, 100, 110, 167
  executions in, 112
The New York Times, 177

Osborne, Thomas Mott, 51

Pakaluk, Michael, 67
Passell, Peter, 124
poor
  death penalty discriminates against,

78, 109, 152-155
  con, 156-159
  legal representation of, 109, 136
Powell, Lewis F., Jr., 130, 134

racism, 78-79, 147, 151
Rantoul, Robert, Jr., 37
Reagan, Ronald, 170
Reese, Charley, 103
Rehnquist, William H., 127, 134
Reinhardt, Stephen, 133
Rice, Charles E., 115
Richardson, James, 64-66

Selby, Pierre Dale, 99
sentence appeals
  thwart capital punishment, 127-132
  con, 133-136
Sourcebook of Criminal Justice Statistics, 149-150
states
  capital punishment laws, 128, 131, 136, 157
  murder rates, 98, 111-112, 124
Steffen, Lloyd, 61
Stephens, Matthew L., 105
Stethem, Robert Dean, 177
Stewart, Potter, 104
Stiglitz, Jan, 135
Sullum, Jacob, 57
Swift, Jonathan, 175

terrorists
  should be executed, 174-177
  con, 178-181
Thomas Aquinas, Saint, 69, 70, 71, 72
Tibbs, Delbert, 108
torture, 18, 179, 181
Traficant, James A., 171

UNITA, 181
United States, 46, 172
  capital punishment laws, 48, 62, 80, 129
  Congress, 129, 134, 170, 172
  Constitution, 170, 172
    capital punishment violates, 87, 110, 173
    con, 128, 167-168
    Fourteenth Amendment, 146
    habeas corpus restrictions violate, 134, 135
    con, 131, 132
  crime in, 42

death row inmates, 63, 106, 150
executions in, 76, 106-107, 124,
  150, 157
Justice Department, 100, 149, 166
murder rates, 43, 50, 106, 124, 157
Supreme Court, 98
  and execution of juveniles, 83,
    87-88, 90
  and racial discrimination, 143,
    146-147, 151
  and sentencing appeals, 100, 101,
    102, 108, 136
  capital punishment cases, 110,
    128, 150, 155, 167, 168, 170, 173

van den Haag, Ernest, 82, 117, 156
Voltaire, François Marie Arouet de,
  23

women, 103-104

Young, John, 109-110

Zimring, Franklin E., 171